Applying the Science of Learning

Richard E. Mayer

University of California, Santa Barbara

PEARSON

Boston   Columbus   Indianapolis   New York   San Francisco   Upper Saddle River
Amsterdam   Cape Town   Dubai   London   Madrid   Milan   Munich   Paris   Montreal   Toronto
Delhi   Mexico City   Sao Paulo   Sydney   Hong Kong   Seoul   Singapore   Taipei   Tokyo

Dedicated to Beverly

Editor-in-Chief: Paul A. Smith
Editorial Assistant: Matthew Buchholz
Associate Editor: Shannon Steed
Vice President, Director of Marketing: Quinn Perkson
Marketing Manager: Jared Brueckner
Production Editor: Gregory Erb
Editorial Production Service: Omegatype Typography, Inc.
Manufacturing Buyer: Megan Cochran
Electronic Composition: Omegatype Typography, Inc.
Interior Design: Omegatype Typography, Inc.
Cover Designer: Linda Knowles

Library of Congress Cataloging-in-Publication Data

Mayer, Richard E.
  Applying the science of learning / Richard E. Mayer.
      p.   cm.
  Includes bibliographical references and index.
  ISBN-13: 978-0-13-611757-5 (pbk.)
  ISBN-10: 0-13-611757-0 (pbk.)
 1. Learning, Psychology of.   2. Educational psychology.
 3. Educational evaluation.   I. Title.
  LB1060.M3395 2011
  370.15'23—dc22

                              2009043397

www.pearsonhighered.com

ISBN-10: 0-13-611757-0
ISBN-13: 978-0-13-611757-5

ABOUT THE AUTHOR

Richard E. Mayer is a professor of psychology at the University of California, Santa Barbara (UCSB), where he has served since 1975. He received a PhD in psychology from the University of Michigan in 1973, and served as a visiting assistant professor of psychology at Indiana University from 1973 to 1975. His research interests are in educational and cognitive psychology. His current research involves the intersection of cognition, instruction, and technology, with a special focus on multimedia learning and computer-supported learning. He is a former president of the Division of Educational Psychology of the American Psychological Association, former editor of the *Educational Psychologist,* former co-editor of *Instructional Science,* former chair of the UCSB Department of Psychology, and the year 2000 recipient of the E. L. Thorndike Award for career achievement in educational psychology. He is the winner of the 2008 Distinguished Contribution of Applications of Psychology to Education and Training Award from the American Psychological Association. He was ranked as the most productive educational psychologist for 1991–2002 (*Contemporary Educational Psychology,* 2003) and for 2003–2008 (*Contemporary Educational Psychology,* 2009). Currently he is vice president for Division C (Learning and Instruction) of the American Educational Research Association. He is on the editorial boards of 14 journals, mainly in educational psychology. He has served as a local school board member in Goleta, California, since 1981. He is the author or editor of more than 400 publications, including 25 books, such as *Multimedia Learning* (2009), *Learning and Instruction* (2008), *E-Learning and the Science of Instruction* (with R. Clark, 2008), and the *Cambridge Handbook of Multimedia Learning* (editor, 2005).

Thinking and Problem Solving (1977)

Foundations of Learning and Memory [with R. Tarpy] (1978)

Human Reasoning [co-editor, with R. Revlin] (1978)

Readings in Learning and Memory [co-editor, with R. Tarpy] (1979)

Ten Statement Spiral BASIC (1980)

The Promise of Cognitive Psychology (1981)

Thinking, Problem Solving, Cognition (1983)

BASIC: A Short Course (1986)

Educational Psychology: A Cognitive Approach (1987)

Teaching and Learning Computer Programming [editor] (1988)

The Critical Thinker: Learning and Thinking Strategies for Psychology Students [with F. Goodchild] (1990)

Thinking, Problem Solving, Cognition (2nd ed.) (1992)

The Critical Thinker: Learning and Thinking Strategies for Psychology Students (2nd ed.) [with F. Goodchild] (1995)

The Promise of Educational Psychology, Volume 1: Learning in the Content Areas (1999)

A Taxonomy of Learning for Teaching: A Revision of Bloom's Taxonomy of Educational Objectives [with L. W. Anderson, D. R. Krathwohl, et al.] (2001)

Multimedia Learning (2001)

The Promise of Educational Psychology, Volume 2: Teaching for Meaningful Learning (2002)

Learning and Instruction (2003)

E-Learning and the Science of Instruction [with R. Clark] (2003)

The Cambridge Handbook of Multimedia Learning [editor] (2005)

E-Learning and the Science of Instruction (2nd ed.) [with R. Clark] (2008)

Learning and Instruction (2nd ed.) (2008)

Multimedia Learning (2nd ed.) (2009)

Applying the Science of Learning (2011)

Handbook of Research on Learning and Instruction [co-editor, with P. Alexander] (2011)

CONTENTS

Section 3   HOW ASSESSMENT WORKS   91

EPILOGUE   127

PREFACE

Applying the Science of Learning

The central mission of education is to help people learn. The science of learning is the scientific study of how people learn. This book attempts to bring these two endeavors together by examining how to apply the science of learning to education. The underlying premise is that if you want to help people learn, it would be useful for you to know something about how learning works. In short, your efforts to improve education will be improved if you strive to apply the science of learning.

Applying the science of learning is not a straightforward one-way process of taking what psychologists have discovered about learning and simply using it to improve the design of instruction. Rather, applying the science of learning involves reciprocal relations among three essential elements—learning, instruction, and assessment. To help you appreciate these interrelations, I have organized this book around these three essential elements: the science of learning, the science of instruction, and the science of assessment.

- *Science of learning.* The first step is to identify the features of a science of learning that are most relevant to education. For much of its 100-year history the science of learning has focused mainly on learning by laboratory animals or humans in contrived laboratory tasks that have little relevance for education. More recently, there have been exciting advances in understanding how people learn in educationally relevant tasks, thereby enabling the construction of a science of learning that is relevant to education. In this book, I highlight for you the features of the science of learning that I think are most relevant to education.
- *Science of instruction.* Second, even if we completely understood how learning works, that understanding would not necessarily translate into prescriptions for instruction. What is needed is a way to test the effectiveness of instructional methods that are suggested by the science of learning, in order to examine when and how they work. This is the task of the science of instruction, whose key features I highlight for you in this book.
- *Science of assessment.* Third, any attempt to apply the science of learning is incomplete without a clear way of assessing what is learned. Clear descriptions of desired learning outcomes are essential for designing instruction and clear descriptions of obtained learning outcomes are essential for evaluating instructional effectiveness. In this book, I highlight the key features of the science of assessment and show you how they are related to improving instruction.

For more than 100 years, psychologists have been trying to figure out how learning works, and for just as long educators have been interested in applying the science of learning to improve education. Throughout most of this period, attempts to apply the science of learning have been less than successful—mainly because most learning research did not focus on explaining how people learn in educationally relevant tasks. However, within the last 25 years, there have been impressive advances in the development of an educationally relevant science of learning. If you are interested in taking a scientific approach to helping people learn, then this book is for you.

My goal in this book is to provide you with an introduction to the foundational ideas in the science of learning, the science of instruction, and the science of assessment. I have designed the book to be:

- *Concise and concentrated.* Instead of trying to cover the content of the field in detail, I am providing you with a sort of executive summary of what I consider to be the foundational ideas in learning, instruction, and assessment. I have worked hard to weed out any unneeded paragraphs, sentences, or even clauses, leaving you with the foundational ideas in concentrated form.
- *Modular and multimedia.* Instead of giving you page after page of running information, I have organized the book in a modular design in which each set of facing pages constitutes a unit with a specific objective. Instead of giving you pages full of words, I have coordinated the text with graphics intended to help you organize and understand the material.
- *Clear and concrete.* I also have worked hard to write in a clear style. I try to be concrete and direct with you, such as by providing definitions and examples of necessary jargon.
- *Personal and friendly.* Instead of writing in a formal, academic style, I have tried to write directly to you as if we were in a friendly conversation. To achieve this goal I have minimized academic references while still providing key references and suggested readings at the end of each section.

Who is this book written for? In writing this book, I envisioned you as someone interested in improving education who has just asked me, "What do I need to know about applying the science of learning?" This book is my humble attempt to answer your question as earnestly as I can, by drawing on my 30-plus years of experience in conducting research on applying the science of learning. In short, if you are interested in what the science of learning has to contribute to improving education, then this book is written for you. I wrote this book for beginners to the science of learning—including undergraduate students in education or psychology, teachers or prospective teachers, and instructional designers or instructors—but I hope it will also be of interest to more experienced readers as well. This book can be used as a supplement to a core textbook in a course (including my *Learning and Instruction,* Second Edition), but it also works as a concise stand-alone introduction to applying the science of learning.

I have been writing this book in my head for years. However, I was finally motivated to put my ideas on paper after recently learning that I had won the Distinguished Contribution of Applications of Psychology to Education and Training Award from the American Psychological Association. Indeed, that surprising event made me realize that it may be time for me to spell out as clearly as possible what I think it means to apply the science of learning. Writing this book has been a delight for me. As any teacher knows, trying to explain something to someone else forces you to work harder to understand it yourself. Such has been my experience in trying to explain to you what it means to apply the science of learning. I hope you will feel free to contact me at mayer@psych.ucsb.edu with your comments and suggestions.

Talks to Teachers

In the late 1800s, the famous American psychologist William James toured the United States giving talks to teachers on how to apply the "science of the mind's laws" to education. His talks were later published in 1899 as a little book, *Talks to Teachers.** Similar to my goal in this book, William James was interested in what it means to apply the science of learning (although, of course, this phrase had not yet been invented) to education.

*James, W. (1899/1958). *Talks to teachers.* New York: Norton. [Originally published in 1899.]

A Psychologist Talks to Teachers in 1899 about Applying the Science of Learning

The desire of the schoolteachers for a completer professional training, and their aspiration toward the professional spirit in their work, have led more and more to turn to us for light on fundamental principles. . . . You look to me . . . for information concerning the mind's operation, which may enable you to labor more easily and effectively in the several classrooms over which you preside. (p. 22)

In his talks to teachers, William James recognized two important obstacles to applying the science of learning. First, learning researchers had not yet developed a science of learning that was educationally relevant.

Problem 1: Is the Science of Learning Educationally Relevant?

Psychology ought certainly give the teacher radical help. And yet I confess that, acquainted as I am with the height of your expectations, I feel a little anxious lest, at the end of these simple talks of mine, not a few of you may experience some disappointment at the net results. (p. 22)

Second, a science of learning does not translate directly into an instructional program. You also need a corresponding science of instruction aimed at determining when and how theory-inspired instructional methods work.

Problem 2: Where Is the Science of Instruction?

You make a great, a very great mistake, if you think that psychology, being the science of the mind's laws, is something from which you can deduce definite programs and schemes and methods of instruction for immediate classroom use. (p. 23)

Today, more than 100 years after *Talks to Teachers*, we finally live in an era with a science of learning that has educational relevance and a science of instruction that has made exciting advances in testing the effectiveness of theory-inspired instructional methods. You can think of the book you are holding as a modern-day version of *Talks to Teachers* that attempts to overcome the obstacles experienced in the past.

Acknowledgments

I appreciate the many helpful comments from the following colleagues who graciously agreed to review the book: Lorin Anderson, Dick Clark, Ruth Clark, Art Graesser, Diane Halpern, Harry O'Neil, and John Sweller. I wish to thank my mentors and teachers as well as the many students and colleagues I have worked with over the years. I am grateful to the University of California, Santa Barbara for providing me with such a wonderful research environment and for surrounding me with bright and energetic students and colleagues. I appreciate the support and encouragement of this book's publisher. I would also like to thank the reviewers of this book, Douglass Kauffman, University of Nebraska, and Stefanie Saccoman, California State—Polytechnic University, Pomona.

Family is very important to me, so I thank my parents, James and Bernis Mayer, who live always in my memory. I thank my children, Ken, Dave, and Sarah, who bring so much joy into my life, and my new grandchildren, Jacob and Avery, who so effortlessly can make me smile. Finally, I thank my wife, Beverly, for making my life so sweet.

Richard E. Mayer
Santa Barbara, California

INTRODUCTION

Helping people learn is a major goal of education. Applying the science of learning refers to using what we know about how people learn to develop research-based instructional methods that help people learn. To accomplish this goal it is useful to understand how learning works (i.e., the science of learning), how instruction works (i.e., the science of instruction), and how assessment works (i.e., the science of assessment). This introduction provides an overview of these three elements.

Bite-Size Chunks of Applying the Science of Learning

The Big Three: Learning, Instruction, and Assessment

Rationale for Applying the Science of Learning

What Is Applying the Science of Learning?

Historical Overview of the Relation between the Science of Learning and the Science of Instruction

Viewing the Relation between the Science of Learning and the Science of Instruction as Overlapping Goals

The Big Three: Learning, Instruction, and Assessment

This book is concerned with taking a scientific approach to how to help people learn. If you want to help people learn, you can get guidance from three main research-based elements:

1. *Science of learning*—which seeks to a create a research-based theory of how learning works,
2. *Science of instruction*—which seeks to identify effective instructional methods that promote learning, and
3. *Science of assessment*—which seeks to create instruments that describe the learner's knowledge, characteristics, and cognitive processing during learning.

I summarize these three elements—learning, instruction, and assessment—in the following figure. Learning is in the center of the figure because learning is in the center of the educational process. The goal of education is to foster a desired change in the learner—this change is called *learning. Instruction* is on the left side with an arrow leading to *learning* because instruction is intended to cause learning. An important task of educators is to employ effective instructional methods that foster change in learners. *Assessment* is on the right side of the figure with an arrow leading from *learning* because assessment provides a description of what was learned (and the cognitive processes that produced the learning). Without some form of assessment, you would not be able to determine whether learning took place. In addition, the arrow from *assessment* back to *instruction* indicates that descriptions of the learner—including what the learner knows and how the learner learns—are useful in planning instruction.

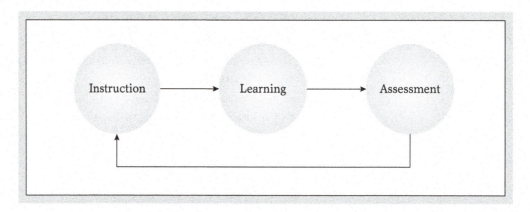

In short, to understand how to improve learning, you need to know about three closely interrelated elements—learning, instruction, and assessment. The remainder of this book is segmented into sections that introduce you to each of these elements.

In this book, I take a scientific approach to learning, instruction, and assessment. The science of learning is concerned with developing a testable theory of how people learn. Learning theories are scientific if they are testable—that is, if it is theoretically possible to find data showing that the theory is false. The science of instruction is concerned with discovering evidence-based methods for helping people learn. Instructional methods are scientific when they are based on research evidence—that is, they have been shown to be effective in methodologically sound studies. The science of assessment is concerned with designing valid and reliable ways to assess learning outcomes, processes, and capabilities. Assessment is scientific when its measurements are valid—that is, they are used for an appropriate purpose—and reliable—that is, they give the same measurement each time we use them.

What is the science of learning?

Definition:	The science of learning is the scientific study of how people learn.
Goal:	Research-based model of how learning works.
Criterion:	Theories are testable.

What is the science of instruction?

Definition:	The science of instruction is the scientific study of how to help people learn.
Goal:	Research-based principles of instructional design indicating which instructional methods work for teaching which kinds of knowledge to which kinds of learners under which kinds of circumstances.
Criterion:	Instructional methods are based on evidence.

What is the science of assessment?

Definition:	The science of assessment is the scientific study of how to determine what people know.
Goal:	Valid and reliable instruments for assessing learning outcomes, learning processes, and learning capabilities.
Criterion:	Instruments are valid and reliable.

Rationale for Applying the Science of Learning

The goal of this book is to help you understand how to help people learn—a goal that involves what I call *applying the science of learning*. To accomplish this goal, you need to understand how learning works, how instruction works, and how assessment works.

Why Learning Is Important

Consider what is special about humans. Why have we been able to survive and prosper as a species? It is not our strength (other animals are stronger), our size (other animals are larger), our speed (other animals are faster), or our camouflage (other animals blend in better with their environments). What makes us special is our extraordinary ability to learn, that is, our ability to build and use knowledge. According to the famous developmental psychologist Jean Piaget, humans construct knowledge in order to survive in the environment. Our mental representations—which we build through learning—help us to get what we want and enable us to survive. In short, the ability to learn is a powerful gift for our species.

Why Instruction Is Important

Every human society has developed ways of exploiting our ability to learn in order to help educate the next generation—that is, to help new members of society build the knowledge they need to survive. Education is our attempt to use the human capacity to learn in ways that improve people's lives. Instruction involves exposing learners to experiences that are intended to promote learning. Instruction can be informal—such as children learning how to behave by observing their parents, siblings, and peers—or formal—such as in schools. Widespread compulsory education is a relatively new institution in human history, only beginning to appear in industrialized societies in the 1800s. If knowledge is the key to success in human societies, then instruction is an important tool for helping people develop that knowledge.

Why Assessment Is Important

Not all instructional experiences are equally effective, so we need ways to determine how and what people learn under different instructional methods. This is the task of assessment. How can we tell whether someone has learned anything? How can we tell what cognitive processes they are using during learning? How can we tell about their capacity to learn? These are questions addressed through assessment. Assessment is important because it allows us to gauge the effectiveness of instruction, and thereby guide the instructional process.

Why Learning, Instruction, and Assessment Are Important	
Element	**Importance**
Learning	Enables us to create knowledge needed for our survival
Instruction	Enhances the learning process
Assessment	Guides the instructional process

What Is Applying the Science of Learning?

Applying the science of learning and invigorating the science of learning are two sides of the same coin. Applying the science of learning means using what we know about how people learn to increase our effectiveness in designing instruction that helps people learn in authentic tasks. In short, it is useful to understand how people learn if your goal is to help people learn.

Invigorating the science of learning refers to expanding learning theory so it is able to account for how learning works in authentic tasks. By the mid-1900s it had become clear that research on how hungry rats run mazes and how bored humans memorize random word lists had failed to create a general theory of learning. There is reason to suspect that learning theory would have died out by the mid-1900s had it not been rescued by the challenges of educational practice. The science of learning was invigorated—perhaps, resuscitated—when educators asked for specific theories of how people learn authentic tasks—such as how to read a passage, how to write an essay, or how to solve arithmetic word problems. In short, if your goal is to understand how people learn, it is useful to examine learning in authentic situations.

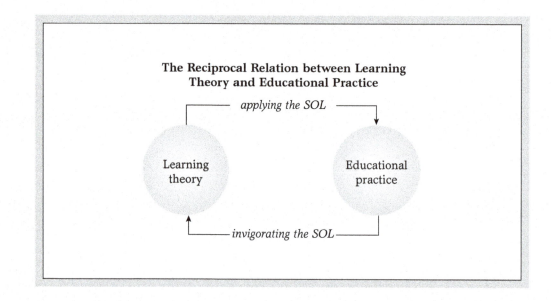

The Reciprocal Relation between Learning Theory and Educational Practice

applying the SOL

Learning theory

Educational practice

invigorating the SOL

Applying and Invigorating the Science of Learning (SOL)	
Goal	Outcome
Applying the SOL	Building an educationally relevant science of learning improves educational practice.
Invigorating the SOL	Seeking to improve educational practice improves the science of learning.

Historical Overview of the Relation between the Science of Learning and the Science of Instruction

Before we examine the big three—learning, instruction, and assessment—it is useful to consider the relations among them, particularly between the science of learning (SOL) and the science of instruction (SOI). The following table summarizes three phases in the relation—one-way street, dead-end street, and two-way street.

Historical Overview of the Relation between the Science of Learning and the Science of Instruction		
Phase	**Time Frame**	**Description**
One-way street	Early 1900s	Basic researchers create the SOL, practitioners apply it.
Dead-end street	Mid-1900s	Basic researchers create learning theory based on contrived learning situations (SOL), which is ignored by applied researchers. Applied researchers create instructional principles that are not grounded in theory (SOI), which are ignored by basic researchers.
Two-way street	Late 1900s and beyond	Researchers test learning theory in authentic learning situations (SOL) and test instructional principles that are grounded in theory (SOI).

Early in the 20th century hopes were high that science would solve society's problems. According to this vision, psychologists would conduct basic research on how learning works and educators would apply the theory in their classrooms. I call this a *one-way street* relation because the line of communication goes only in one direction—from learning theory to educational practice. The one-way street approach was not successful for two main reasons: (a) Psychologists of the day were not able to develop consensus on a theory of learning, and (b) even if psychologists could create a theory of learning, such a theory would not translate directly into educational practice.

By mid-century, the relation had deteriorated into what I call a *dead-end street*, with basic researchers studying how learning works in contrived lab situations such as with rats running in mazes or humans memorizing random lists of words, and applied researchers focusing on which method of instruction was best without any consideration of how instruction worked. During this period, there was not much communication between psychologists working on the science of learning and educators interested in the science of instruction.

In the second half of the 20th century, the lines of communication began to open in a more reciprocal way. Educators challenged learning theorists to develop theories that could explain learning in authentic tasks, such as learning how to read, how to write, how to solve arithmetic problems, or how to think scientifically. In attempting to answer these questions, researchers in the science of learning were able to develop much more powerful and useful theories of learning. The science of instruction benefited by the development of more effective tests of instructional methods, with grounding in how each method affected cognitive processing in the learner. I use the term *two-way street* to refer to this new reciprocal relation between the science of learning and the science of instruction. In my opinion, the two-way street offers the most promise for both the science of learning and the science of instruction.

Let's consider examples of what was happening in the science of learning (SOL) and the science of instruction (SOI) during each phase in the relation.

Examples of the Relation between the Science of Learning and the Science of Instruction

Phase	Example Issues in the SOL	Example Issue in the SOI
One-way street	Animals learn to press a bar to get food in a lab.	Students are taught to answer questions by drill and practice.
Dead-end street	What are the laws of learning based on word lists?	Do students learn to read better with phonics or the whole word method?
Two-way street	What are the principles of learning to read?	How can we help students learn to read?

For example, in the one-way street phase, psychologists studied how rewards and punishments affected response learning in lab animals, and educators applied the findings by using drill-and-practice methods to teach students how to answer factual questions. For example, the student received a reward (such as the teacher saying "Right") for a correct answer and a punishment (such as the teacher saying "Wrong") for an incorrect answer. In the dead-end street phase, psychologists continued to conduct learning research in contrived lab environments—such as determining the principles underlying how people learn word lists—while educators, for example, compared two different methods of how to teach reading without having a theoretical basis for how they worked. Finally, during the two-way street period, psychologists broadened their focus to the study of learning of authentic tasks, such as how children learn to read, while educators, for example, focused on how to help students learn to read based on evidence and a theoretical grounding in how the methods affect learning. Today, progress is being made along the two-way street. In fact, the growth of a multidisciplinary approach to cognitive science suggests that we are moving along a multilane superhighway with lanes for multiple disciples as well as on and off ramps for varied learning goals.

Viewing the Relation between the Science of Learning and the Science of Instruction as Overlapping Goals

There is much confusion about the nature of *basic research* (exemplified by the science of learning) and *applied research* (exemplified by the science of instruction). In his book, *Pasteur's Quadrant*, Donald Stokes helps dispel this confusion by delineating four possible research goals that researchers can have:

- Only a theoretical goal (indicated in the bottom left quadrant of the following figure as pure basic research)
- Only a practical goal (indicated in the top right quadrant as pure applied research)
- Neither goal (indicated in the top left quadrant as an empty cell)
- Both goals (indicated in the bottom right quadrant as basic research on applied problems)

In this fourth quadrant of *Pasteur's Quadrant*, which Donald Stokes refers to as *use-inspired basic research*, researchers have two overlapping goals. For example, in adapting Stokes' analysis to educational research, the following table contains a quadrant in which researchers seek to contribute to learning theory and to instructional practice. It is in this quadrant that important advances can be made both in learning theory—by creating theories that apply to authentic learning situations—and in instructional practice—by understanding when and how instructional methods work. This quadrant corresponds to a two-way street between basic and applied research, in which the lines of communication are reciprocal.

As shown in the table at the right, there are two ways of conceptualizing the relation between basic research (such as the science of learning) and applied research (such as the science of instruction): as *two poles on a continuum* or as *two overlapping goals*. The conventional view is that applied research and basic research are two poles on a continuum such that the science of learning (i.e., viewed as basic research on one side) focuses on the theoretical question of how people learn and the science of instruction (i.e., viewed as applied research on the other side) focuses on the practical question of how to produce effective instruction. The undesirable consequence of

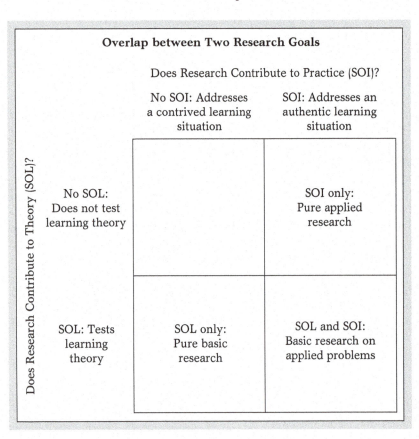

Overlap between Two Research Goals

Does Research Contribute to Practice (SOI)?

Does Research Contribute to Theory (SOL)?	No SOI: Addresses a contrived learning situation	SOI: Addresses an authentic learning situation
No SOL: Does not test learning theory		SOI only: Pure applied research
SOL: Tests learning theory	SOL only: Pure basic research	SOL and SOI: Basic research on applied problems

the poles-on-a-continuum view is that learning researchers are guided to develop theories that do not apply to authentic tasks whereas instructional researchers are encouraged to develop instructional methods that are not grounded in theory and thus have limited applicability. In contrast, I prefer the overlapping goals view in which it is possible to conduct research that addresses two goals simultaneously—contributing to the science of learning by building a theory of how people learn and contributing to the science of instruction by discovering research-based principles for how to design effective instruction. The desirable consequence of this view is that research can result in more authentic theories of learning and more widely applicable instructional methods.

Two Views of Basic (SOL) and Applied (SOI) Research

View	Description	Consequence
Two poles on a continuum	Basic research concerns theory; applied research concerns practice.	Theories do not apply to authentic tasks; practical principles are not grounded in theory.
Two overlapping goals	Basic research on applied problems (i.e., research contributes to theory and practice).	Theories are informed by evidence from authentic tasks; practical principles are grounded in theory.

If we seek research with overlapping goals (as shown on the right side of the following illustration), we enter the realm of what I call *basic research on applied problems* (or what Stokes calls *use-inspired basic research*). When we work in this quadrant, the distinction between basic research and applied research disappears because good applied research and good basic research become the same thing. In this quadrant we create a reciprocal relation between the science of learning and the science of instruction. This is the quadrant in which this book is situated.

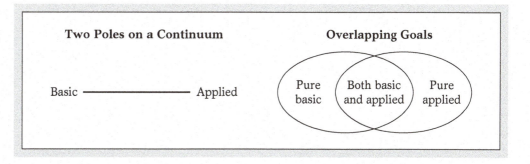

References and Suggested Readings

Pages 4–5

Piaget, J. (1971). *Science of education and the psychology of the child.* New York: Viking Press.

A description of the relation between psychology and education by the world's leading developmental psychologist.

Pages 8–9

Mayer, R. E. (2008). *Learning and instruction* (2nd ed). Upper Saddle River, NJ: Merrill/Pearson Prentice Hall.

An up-to-date review of key concepts in educational psychology and an analysis of the history of the relation between psychology and education.

Pages 10–11

Stokes, D. E. (1997). *Pasteur's quadrant: Basic science and technological innovation.* Washington, DC: Brookings Institution Press.

An eloquent plea for the idea that the same research project can make theoretical contributions (e.g., to the science of learning) as well as practical contributions (e.g., to the science of instruction).

Section 1 How Learning Works

Education is concerned with fostering productive changes in learners. These changes are called learning.

If you want to help people learn, it would be helpful for you to understand how learning works. In short, the instructional methods you use to promote learning should be consistent with what we know about how the human mind works. This is the premise underlying this section of the book.

In this section, I provide a brief overview of how learning works by exploring each of the subtopics listed below.

Bite-Size Chunks of the Science of Learning

What Is Learning?

Learning is a change in knowledge attributable to experience. This definition has three main parts—(1) learning involves a change in the learner, (2) what is changed is the learner's knowledge, and (3) the cause of the change is the learner's experience.

Learning is a change in knowledge attributable to experience.

Learning

1. is a change

2. in what the learner knows

3. caused by the learner's experience

Let's examine those three parts in more detail. First, what happens when you learn? Learning always involves change. The change takes place within the learner and is long-lasting. When you learn, you are changed. If you have not changed, you have not learned. As you can see, change is the central idea in learning.

Second, what changes when you learn? There is a change in what you know, that is, in your knowledge. I am using the term *knowledge* in a broad sense to include *facts, procedures, concepts, strategies,* and *beliefs.* A change in knowledge can never be directly detected but instead can be inferred by observing a change in the learner's behavior (such as answers on a test).

Third, what causes learning to happen? Learning is caused by the learner's experience in the environment. The learning process is initiated when a learner interacts with his or her environment—such as through participating in a discussion, reading a book chapter, or playing an educational game. The ability to learn from our experience is an extremely useful characteristic for our species, because it contributes to our survival. In education, we take this aspect of learning one step further by intentionally creating learning environments. When we arrange the learner's environment in ways that are intended to promote changes in the learner's knowledge, we are providing instruction—a topic explored in Section 2 of this book.

If you checked the first line, I would say that you are right. Andy displays a change in his knowledge about how to play the game (as indicated by a change in his scores) due to his experience (in playing a video game). Similarly, if you checked the second line, you are consistent with the way I interpret the definition of *learning*. Based on his experience with cute little Buddy, John shows a change in his knowledge—broadly defined as his beliefs about dogs. However, these are the only check marks I'd like to see.

You might be tempted to check the third line because it involves a change in what Pat knows (i.e., the first two elements in the definition), but it is caused by an external physical intervention rather than by experience (i.e., the third element in the definition).

You also might be tempted to check the fourth line because it involves a change in what Sue knows at least as measured by her exam performance (i.e., the first two elements in the definition), but it is caused by an external chemical intervention rather than by experience (i.e., the third element in the definition).

The fifth example may appeal to you because it involves a change—a reduction in speed on solving math problems—but the change is in Sarah's performance rather than her knowledge (i.e., the second element in the definition) and the change is caused by Sarah's fatigue rather than by her experience (i.e., the third element in the definition).

Finally, the sixth example about Mark's quiz show performance has one of the elements in the definition of learning (i.e., a change in the learner), but the change is in Mark's performance rather than his knowledge (i.e., the second element) and the change is caused by Mark's motivation rather than his experience in the environment (i.e., the third element).

Overall, each scenario involves a change in the learner but in the last four the change is not attributable to experience and in the last two the change is not even in what the learner knows.

What Changes:
Behavior or Knowledge?

As shown in the following table, a major controversy in the learning sciences concerns the issue of what changes as a result of learning—the learner's behavior or the learner's knowledge. The consensus throughout much of the first half of the 20th century through the 1950s was that learning involved a change in the learner's behavior. The rationale is that science should focus on observable events such as behavior rather than unobservable events such as knowledge. The consensus since that time has been that learning is a change in the learner's knowledge, which can be inferred by observing changes in the learner's behavior. The rationale is that the knowledge-based view of learning is more useful in explaining complex learning in humans, which goes beyond response learning in laboratory animals.

Behaviorist and Cognitive Views of What Is Learned		
Learning Framework	**What Changes**	**Rationale**
Behaviorist view	Learner's behavior	Behavior is directly observable
Cognitive view	Learner's knowledge	Knowledge is inferred from behavior

As you can see in the figure on the right, the top row shows the behaviorist view of learning in which events in the environment (such as getting rewarded for turning right in a maze) cause changes in behavior (becoming more likely to turn right in the maze in the future).

The bottom row shows the cognitive view in which a new element is added—the learner's cognitive system. What happens in the environment is interpreted and represented in the learner's cognitive system as knowledge, which becomes apparent through the learner's behavior.

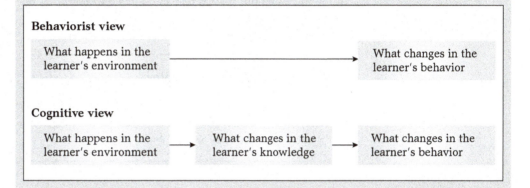

Behaviorist view

What happens in the learner's environment ⟶ What changes in the learner's behavior

Cognitive view

What happens in the learner's environment ⟶ What changes in the learner's knowledge ⟶ What changes in the learner's behavior

Thus, both behaviorists and cognitivists are interested in changes in the learner's performance, but cognitivists have the added task of making inferences about changes in the learner's knowledge (i.e., facts, concepts, procedures, strategies, or beliefs). I take a cognitive view in this book.

What Is the Science of Learning?

In the introduction, we defined the science of learning, but in this section let's elaborate on that definition.

What is the science of learning?

Definition: The science of learning is the scientific study of how people learn.
Goal: Research-based model of how learning works.
Criterion: Theories are testable.

The science of learning is the scientific study of how people learn. What makes it scientific is that it is based on evidence rather than opinions, slogans, or quotations from experts.

The goal of the science of learning is to create a research-based model of how learning works. What makes a theory research-based is that it is based on evidence rather than opinions, slogans, or quotations from experts.

The main criterion of an explanation of how learning works is that it be testable. What makes a theory testable is that you can draw predictions and compare them to research evidence rather than opinions, slogans, or quotations from experts.

As you can see, empirical evidence is at the heart of the science of learning. Learning theories should be based on evidence—this is what I mean by *evidence-based learning theory*. The central role of empirical evidence is eloquently stated in a recent report of the National Research Council edited by Richard Shavelson and Lisa Towne, entitled *Scientific Research in Education*.

> The final court of appeal of the viability of a scientific hypothesis or conjecture is its empirical adequacy. . . . [T]estability and refutability of scientific claims or hypotheses is an important feature of scientific investigations that is not typical in other forms of inquiry. (p. 3)

What are the characteristics of a testable statement? You should be able to collect data that can determine whether or not the statement is true. In particular, you should be able to clearly identify the instructional features and how they are measured. For example, consider the following four statements about how learning works, each of which appears to espouse a constructivist perspective. Please place a check mark next to each statement that is testable.

> **Which Statements Are Testable?**
>
> Place a check mark next to each statement that is testable:
>
> ____ Learners actively construct their own knowledge.
>
> ____ Learning is a sense-making activity.
>
> ____ People who are active during learning learn better than people who are passive.
>
> ____ People who spontaneously generate self-explanations as they read a science text learn more deeply than people who do not.

The first two statements are so vague that they do not suggest what data you could collect to test them. The third statement represents a move in the right direction but still is too vague concerning what it means to be active or passive during learning. The fourth statement deserves a check mark because it is more specific about how to collect evidence, but, of course, there is still room to clarify how self-generation and learning outcomes will be measured. Thus, the fourth statement appears to be a testable hypothesis; the others describe a general framework but are not in testable form. In testing the fourth statement, you would be testing a prediction that is consistent with the constructivist perspective and helps to clarify it. Stating your hypothesis in a testable way is an important step in the science of learning.

A Look at Transfer

What Is Transfer?

Transfer is the effect of prior learning on new learning or performance. How does what you have already learned affect your ability to accomplish a new task? This is the issue of transfer.

> **Transfer is the effect of prior learning on new learning.**
>
> Transfer occurs when:
>
> 1. something you know from prior learning
> 2. affects your performance on a new task.

How Do We Measure Transfer?

The accompanying table shows that we allow the treatment group to have a learning experience—labeled A—such as taking a course in Latin, and we do not allow the control group (which is equivalent) to do so. Then, we give both groups a new task—labeled B—such as taking a course in Spanish.

Testing for Transfer

	Learning Task	Transfer Task
Treatment group	A	B
Control group	—	B

As you can see, if the treatment group accomplishes the transfer task better than the control group, then we have evidence of *positive transfer*—which is a primary goal of education. If the treatment group performs worse on the transfer task than the control group, then we can say that the learning task creates *negative transfer*—which we seek to avoid in education.

Three Kinds of Transfer

Kind of Transfer	Performance on Transfer Task
Positive transfer	Treatment group performs better than control group
Negative transfer	Control group performs better than treatment group
Neutral transfer	Treatment and control groups perform equivalently

What Is General and Specific Transfer?

As shown in the following table, a major controversy in the learning sciences concerns whether learning is specific—so only specific transfer is possible—or general—so general transfer is possible.

Is Transfer Specific or General?		
Breadth of Transfer	**Description**	**Example**
Specific transfer	Specific behaviors (or procedures or facts) in A are like those required in B.	Latin has some similar verb conjugations and words as Spanish, so learning Latin will help you learn Spanish.
General transfer	Although there is nothing in common between A and B, learning A is a mind-enriching experience.	Latin improves the mind so learning Latin should help you solve logic problems.
Mixed transfer	The same general principle or strategy is required in A and B	Learning how to pronounce printed words helps you pronounce words in Latin and Spanish.

Over the past 100 years learning scientists have provided ample evidence for *specific transfer*—when you practice on a specific task you wind up being better able to accomplish that task; but they have not been highly successful in providing evidence for *general transfer*—when you practice on a specific task you generally do not wind up being able to accomplish completely different kinds of tasks. For example, in an early transfer experiment, E. L. Thorndike and his colleagues showed that learning Latin did not help students learn other school subjects, so there was no evidence that Latin fostered general transfer by somehow improving the mind in general. However, more recent research on strategy instruction reported by Michael Pressley and his colleagues shows that students can learn general strategies or principles (such as how to monitor their reading comprehension or how to outline text lessons), which can be used to help them in a variety of tasks (e.g., in reading various kinds of materials). This is evidence for specific transfer of general principles and strategies—which can be called *mixed transfer*.

Overall, the current consensus is that learning can be broader than specific transfer and probably is narrower than general transfer. The key to promoting mixed transfer is to identify strategies and principles that can be used in a broad variety of tasks. For example, in reading, the general concept of rhetorical structures (such as compare and contrast or classification or steps in a process) helps students comprehend a broad variety of expository texts; in mathematics, the general concept of a mental number line helps students learn a broad variety of arithmetic procedures; in science, the general concept of control of variables in scientific experimentation helps students learn to evaluate a variety of scientific hypotheses. In short, learning appears to be somewhat domain specific but there are general principles or strategies that can apply within a particular domain.

How Learning Works:
Three Metaphors of Learning

For more than 100 years, learning scientists have sought to characterize how learning works. Over these years, they have developed three major metaphors of learning—*response strengthening, information acquisition,* and *knowledge construction.* The table on the right compares the three metaphors of learning in terms of the conception of how learning works, role of the learner, role of the teacher, and initial dates of strong impact.

Response Strengthening

Learning involves the strengthening or weakening of an association between a stimulus (such as "What is 2 plus 2?") and a response (such as "4"). The teacher's role is to elicit a response (such as by asking "What is 2 plus 2?") and then administer a reward (such as saying "Right" if the learner says "4") or punishment (such as saying "Wrong" if the learner says "5"). The learner's role is to receive the rewards (which automatically strengthen the association) and punishments (which automatically weaken the association). The underlying idea is that responses that are followed by satisfaction become more strongly associated with the situation so they are more likely to occur in the future; responses that are followed by dissatisfaction become less associated with the situation so they are less likely to occur in the future. The response strengthening metaphor became popular in the early 1900s, and is still a main theoretical framework today, particularly for teaching of skills using drill and practice.

Information Acquisition

Learning involves adding input information (such as "The three metaphors of learning are response strengthening, information acquisition, and knowledge construction") to your memory. The teacher's role is to present the information (such as a lecture, book, or online presentation) and the learner's role is to receive the information for storage. This conception of how learning works is sometimes called the *transmission model* because the teacher transmits information that the learner receives. Similarly, it is sometimes call the *empty vessel model* because the learner's memory is an empty container to be filled with the teacher's information. The information acquisition metaphor became popular in the mid-1900s and is still a main theoretical framework today, particularly for teaching of basic facts.

Knowledge Construction

Learning involves building a mental representation (such as a mental model of how learning works) from which you can make inferences. According to this view, active learning occurs when the learner engages in appropriate cognitive processing during learning. The learner's role is to make sense of the presented material, whereas the teacher's role is to serve as a cognitive guide who helps direct the learner's cognitive processing during learning. The knowledge construction metaphor became popular in the late 1900s and is still the dominant theoretical framework today, particularly for teaching of concepts and strategies.

Three Metaphors of Learning

Name	Conception	Learner's Role	Teacher's Role	Dates
Response strengthening	Strengthening or weakening of an association	Passive recipient of rewards and punishments	Dispenser of rewards and punishments	Early 1900s
Information acquisition	Adding information to memory	Passive recipient of information	Dispenser of information	Mid-1900s
Knowledge construction	Building cognitive representations	Active sense maker	Cognitive guide	Late 1900s

Each metaphor of learning is based on research, each has had an impact on the science of learning, and each has influenced educational practice. Although they have been around for decades, each metaphor continues to have an influence on learning theory and educational practice. Response strengthening may be most relevant for learning of cognitive skills; information acquisition may be most relevant for learning of facts; and knowledge construction may be most relevant for learning concepts and strategies. For purposes of this book, I am focusing mainly on the third metaphor—knowledge construction—because I am most interested in how to promote meaningful learning.

A Closer Look at Response Strengthening: Thorndike's Law of Effect

As an example of evidence for the response strengthening view, let's begin with the first experiments conducted by the world's first educational psychologist, E. L. Thorndike. You can read more about this research in *Animal Intelligence* by E. L. Thorndike, published in 1911.

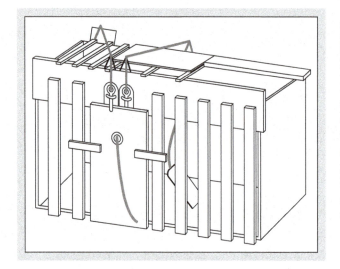

What Was the Method?

In an early study of how learning works reported in 1911, E. L. Thorndike placed a hungry cat into a puzzle box as shown in the figure. As you can see, there is a loop of string connected to a door and a bowl of food placed just outside the puzzle box. The cat had to pull on the loop of string to open a door that would allow the cat to get out and eat a nearby bowl of food. Thorndike placed the cat in the puzzle box each day for a series of days (such as 24 days) and carefully observed what the cat did and how long it took to pull the string to get out.

What Were the Results?

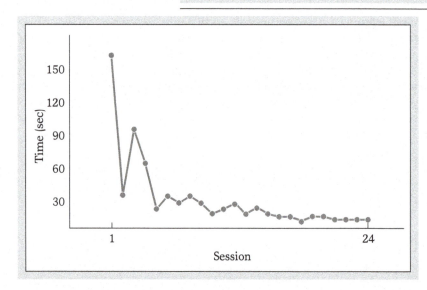

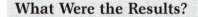

On the first day, the cat engaged in many extraneous behaviors such as trying to jam its paws through the slats of the puzzle box, pouncing on the walls of the puzzle box, and meowing loudly. After about 3 minutes in the puzzle box, the cat accidentally caught its paw in the loop of string, which opened the door so the cat could get out and eat the food. On the next day, the cat engaged in fewer extraneous behaviors and took less time to pull on the loop of string. Over the course of 24 days, the number of extraneous behaviors decreased as did the time it took the cat to get out. The accompanying figure shows the learning curve for one cat. The x-axis shows the sessions (from day 1 to day 24) and the y-axis shows the time for the cat to pull the string and get out (in seconds). As you can see there is a reduction in the time it took to get out of the puzzle box over the days, indicating that the cat was learning. This was one of the first scientific results showing a mathematical relation between amount of practice (indicated by the number of trials indicated on the x-axis) and amount of learning (indicated by a change in solution time on the y-axis).

What Is the Explanation?

The third step in Thorndike's research program was to offer a compelling explanation for the learning curve he obtained. When the cat entered the puzzle box for the first time, it came with what he called a *habit family hierarchy,* as shown in the figure. The habit family hierarchy contained stimulus-response (S-R) associations, such as an association between the stimulus of being confined and hungry and the response of pouncing against the wall. The S-R associations—also called *habits*—formed a family because they all had the same stimulus—namely being in a confined area and hungry. They formed a hierarchy because the responses varied in how strongly they were associated with the stimulus.

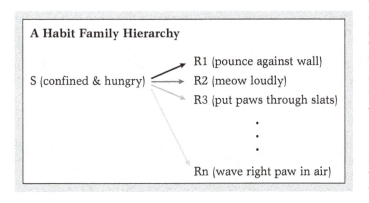

A Habit Family Hierarchy

S (confined & hungry)
- R1 (pounce against wall)
- R2 (meow loudly)
- R3 (put paws through slats)
  .
  .
  .
- Rn (wave right paw in air)

The first time the cat was put in the puzzle box, the cat executed the top response on the hierarchy—such as pouncing. That did not result in getting out so its association was weakened. After several pounces, the association became so weak that the next response (such as meowing) was now at the top of hierarchy, so the cat executed that response. That did not work either so it was weakened. After many attempts, each of the top responses had been tried repeatedly and weakened each time it failed. Eventually, the cat got down to a lower response, such as waving its paw in the air, which resulted in pulling the loop of string and getting out. This association—between being in the puzzle box and pulling the loop of string—was then strengthened. The habit family hierarchy slowly changed with unsuccessful responses becoming weaker each time they failed and the successful response becoming stronger each time it succeeded. Thorndike called this the *law of effect,* which he explained in the following definition.

Law of Effect

Of the several responses made to the same situation, those which are accompanied or closely followed by satisfaction to the animal will, other things being equal, be more firmly connected with the situation so that when it recurs, they will be more likely to recur; those which are accompanied or closely followed by discomfort to the animal will, other things being equal, have their connections with that situation weakened, so that, when it recurs, they will be less likely to occur. The greater the satisfaction or discomfort, the greater the strengthening or weakening of the bond. (p. 244)

After completing this line of research with cats, dogs, and chickens, Thorndike moved on to studying how the law of effect worked with adults and eventually with students learning school subjects. The law of effect is the basis for drill-and-practice methods of instruction, which became popular in the early 1900s and are still commonly used today. The famous learning psychologist B. F. Skinner built on this work to establish his behaviorist approach to learning.

A Closer Look at Information Acquisition: Ebbinghaus' Learning Curve

"From the most ancient subject, we shall produce the newest science." So begins Herman Ebbinghaus' classic book, *Memory,* originally published in German in 1885. In it he describes the first experimental study of learning and memory. If you are looking for the start of the science of learning, Ebbinghaus' book is for you.

What Was The Method?

Read aloud the letter triplets in the following row at a rate of one triplet per second. If you have a metronome—used for keeping time when playing a musical instrument—set it to click every second.

    TOR   NIS   DUL   XAB   VEQ   NIZ   REH   MAF   POS

Now, close the book, count aloud to 30, and try to write down all the triplets in order. This gives you a flavor of the research method used by Ebbinghaus (although he spoke German and used a different testing method). First he constructed lists of nonsense syllables—each consisting of a consonant-vowel-consonant combination that was not a word. Second, he devised a method called *serial learning,* in which he read the list over at a constant rate of one nonsense syllable at a time with the goal of remembering them in order. He repeated this studying for a predetermined schedule of trials (or until he reached mastery) and then tested himself after a predetermined interval. Third, he invented a test of learning outcome called *savings in relearning,* in which he determined the number of trials it took him to relearn the list to mastery. The difference between the number of trials it took to learn initially and the number of trials it took to relearn is called *savings in relearning.*

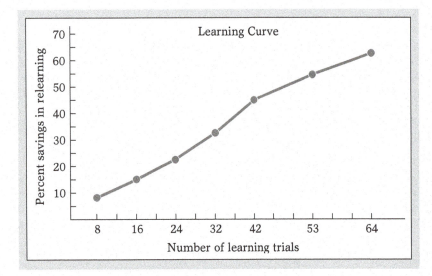

What Were the Results?

The figure shows a learning curve with the number of learning trials on the x-axis (i.e., how many times the list was studied) and percent saved in relearning on a test 24 hours later on the y-axis (i.e., based on how long it took to relearn the list to criterion on the test compared to the initial learning time of 1270 seconds). Ebbinghaus was the first to demonstrate a quantitative relation between the amount of practice and the amount learned.

The next figure shows a forgetting curve with the time since learning on the x-axis and the percent saved in relearning on the *y*-axis (based on a list of 13 nonsense syllables that originally took an average of 1090 seconds to learn to criterion). As you can see, memory falls off rapidly over time. Ebbinghaus was the first to demonstrate a quantitative relation between time since learning and amount remembered.

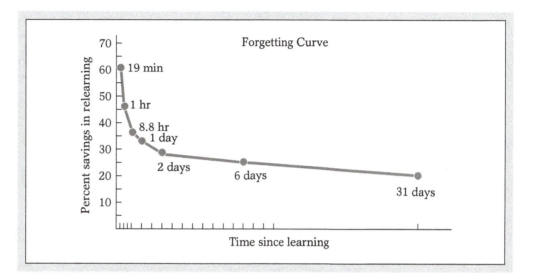

What Is the Explanation?

Ebbinghaus was concerned with factors that influence how much you know. The learning curve shows that the amount you know depends on the amount of practice you put in on learning the material, and the forgetting curve shows that the amount you know depends on the time since learning. As you can see, Ebbinghaus assumed an information acquisition view of learning in which learning was seen as a process of storing information in memory. In a nutshell, here is Ebbinghaus' conception of how learning works:

> As the number of repetitions increases, the series is engraved more and more deeply and indelibly. (p. 53)

Ebbinghaus set the tone for highly rigorous research using controlled experiments and quantitative measurements, all aimed at determining which factors can increase the amount learned. His focus on learning as information acquisition is still influential today and is reflected in instructional methods that present as much information as possible to learners. For example, you may be familiar with thick textbooks overflowing with facts and lectures crammed with fast-paced PowerPoint slides that are full of words.

A Closer Look at Knowledge Construction: Bartlett's Assimilation to Schema

As an example of evidence for the knowledge construction view, let's consider a classic study conducted by Frederick Bartlett, published in his 1932 book *Remembering*.

What Was the Method?

Bartlett asked a British college student to read an unfamiliar folk story from a Native American culture and after a 15 to 30 minute interval to reproduce the story from memory. The reproduced version was given to another college student who read and reproduced it, and so on down the line for a total of 10 reproductions, as in the playground game of telephone. As shown below, the story, called "The War of the Ghosts," describes how two mortals encountered characters from the spirit world, who were about to start an attack.

The War of the Ghosts

One night, two young men from Euglac went down to the river to hunt seals, and while they were there it became foggy and calm. Then they heard war cries and they thought, "Maybe this is a war party." They escaped to the shore, and hid behind a log. Now the canoes came up, and they heard the sound of paddles, and saw one canoe coming up to them. There were five men in the canoe and they said: "What do you think? We wish to take you along. We are going up the river to make war on the people."

One of the men said: "I have no arrows."

"Arrows are in the canoe," they said.

"I will not go along. I might get killed. My relatives do not know where I have gone. But you," he said, turning to the other, "may go with them."

So one of the young men went, but the other returned home.

And the warriors went up the river to a town on the other side of Kalama. The people came out to the water, and they began to fight, and many were killed. But presently the young man heard one of the warriors say: "Quick, let's go home: the Indian has been hit." Now he thought, "Oh, they are ghosts." He did not feel sick, but they said he was shot.

So the canoes went back to Egulac, and the young man went ashore to his house, and made a fire. And he told everybody and said: "Behold I was accompanied by the ghosts, and they went to fight. Many of our fellows were killed, and many of those who attacked us were killed. They said I was hit, and I did not feel sick."

He told it all, and then became quiet. When the sun rose he fell down. Something black came out of his mouth. His face became contorted. The people jumped up and cried. He was dead.

What Were the Results?

By the time the story was reproduced by the last (tenth) person in line, it turned into a shorter and more coherent story (i.e., more coherent from the learner's perspective). As you can see, the theme concerning the intrusion of the spirit world (which is unfamiliar to the learner) is completely lost, and the theme of a war story (which is familiar to the learner) is substituted as an organizing framework. Details inconsistent with the war theme are lost whereas consistent new details are invented.

The War of the Ghosts

Two Indians were out fishing for seals in the Bay of Manpapan, when along came five other Indians in a war-canoe. They were going fighting.

"Come with us," said the five to the two, "and fight."

"I cannot come," was the answer of one, "for I have an old mother at home who is dependent on me." The other also said he could not come, because he had no arms. "That's no difficulty," the others replied, "for we have plenty in the canoe with us"; so he got into the canoe and went with them.

In a fight soon afterwards this Indian received a mortal wound. Finding that his hour was come, he cried out that he was about to die. "Nonsense," said one of the others, "you will not die." But he did.

In examining the series of 10 reproduced versions of the story, Bartlett noticed that the story changed in systematic ways, which he called *leveling, sharpening,* and *rationalization* as shown in the following table.

Three Cognitive Processes in Learning and Remembering		
Name	**Description**	**Example**
Leveling	Losing specific details	Location changes from "Egulac" to "Bay of Manpapan"
Sharpening	Elaborating certain crucial details	Changing "My relatives do not know where I have gone" to "I have an old mother at home who is dependent on me"
Rationalization	Reorganizing the story around a familiar theme	Changing from a story about a spirit world to a story about a war battle

What Is the Explanation?

Bartlett proposed that meaningful learning involves assimilating new incoming information to existing schemas. A schema is an organizing structure that connects knowledge elements into a coherent mental representation. British college students did not have schemas concerning the kind of spirit world involved in the story, so they assimilated the "War of the Ghosts" story to a more familiar (though inappropriate) schema—such as a war battle. According to Bartlett, learning is impaired when a learner lacks the appropriate prior knowledge, because the outcome of learning depends both on what is presented and the learner's existing knowledge used to assimilate it. In this way learning is a constructive process of *assimilation to schema* rather than a process of adding presented information to memory. Concerning remembering, Bartlett proposed that the learner mentally reconstructs the story based on remembering a general organizing schema—such as a war battle—and a few fragments of the story. In this way remembering is an act of reconstruction rather that a process of information retrieval. As you can see, Bartlett was one of the first to propose a constructivist alternative to the information acquisition view that information is added to memory during learning and retrieved during remembering. In short, Bartlett offered the vision of learners as active sense makers and provided supporting evidence.

How Learning Works: Three Principles from the Learning Sciences

If you want to help people learn, it would be useful for you to know something about how the human information processing system works. In the following table I summarize three fundamental research-based principles from the science of learning—*dual channels, limited capacity,* and *active processing.* Any useful theory of learning has to include these three basic principles.

Three Principles from the Science of Learning	
Principle	**Definition**
Dual channels	People have separate channels for processing verbal and visual material.
Limited capacity	People can process only small amounts of material in each channel at any one time.
Active processing	Meaningful learning occurs when learners engage in appropriate cognitive processing during learning (such as attending to relevant material, organizing it into a coherent representation, and integrating it with relevant prior knowledge).

Dual Channels Principle

We start with the idea that humans possess two separate channels for processing information—a verbal channel that we use for processing verbal material and a visual channel that we use for visual material. Words and pictures are processed in different parts of the brain, and are represented differently in the human mind.

Limited Capacity Principle

Perhaps the single most important idea in the science of learning is that people can process only a small amount of material in each channel at any one time. These limitations on working memory capacity have important implications for how learning works. Incoming information cannot all fit within working memory so people need to be selective in paying attention to relevant material and trying to make sense of it. People cannot be tape recorders that take in and record vast amounts of material because of our limited processing capacity.

Active Processing

Finally, the third major principle is that meaningful learning occurs when learners engage in appropriate cognitive processing during learning. Active processing includes attending to relevant material, mentally organizing the selected material into a coherent representation, and integrating it with prior knowledge activated from long-term memory.

A Closer Look at Dual Channels: Paivio's Concreteness Effect

Please read the following list of words at the rate of one word every 2 seconds. When you come to the end of the list, close the book and write down all the words you can remember within a time limit of 30 seconds.

Try It!   tree   piano   river   truck   elbow   missile   hammer   caterpillar   book   potato

Next, please read the following list of words at the rate of one word every 2 seconds. When you come to the end of the list, close the book and write down all the words you can remember within 30 seconds.

Try It!   style   effort   quality   truth   encore   irony   tribute   exclusion   namesake   cost

If you are like most people, you probably did better recalling the words in the first list than the words in the second list. This is called the *concreteness effect* because words in the first list are concrete and words in the second list are abstract. How do we know the words are concrete or abstract? When people are asked to rate words like those in the first list on a scale from 1 (very abstract) to 7 (very concrete), these words get a high rating. When people are asked to rate words like those on the second list on the same scale, these words get a low rating.

Please rate this word: TREE

Try It!

1	2	3	4	5	6	7
very abstract						very concrete

In his classic 1971 book *Imagery and Verbal Processes,* Allan Paivio explains how the concreteness effect supports the idea that people have separate information channels for words and pictures. When a learner receives a concrete word such as *tree,* the learner can encode the word verbally and pictorially (by forming a mental image of a tree). Allan Paivio points to evidence showing that it is easier to form mental images for concrete words than for abstract words. In contrast, when a learner receives an abstract word, the learner can encode the word verbally but is less likely to be able to encode the word pictorially. According to Paivio's dual code theory, people learn better when they use two codes to represent incoming information rather than one. A similar piece of evidence is the *picture superiority effect:* an item is better remembered if it is presented as a picture rather than as a word.

A Closer Look at Limited Capacity: Miller's Magic Number 7

Please briefly look at each box and immediately tell how many dots you think are in the box. Do not take the time to count the dots. Just look and say a number, and then move on to the next one.

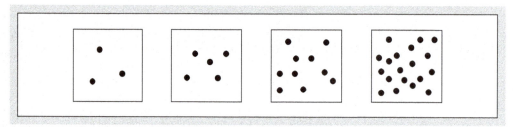

This is called an *attention span* task, because it tells how much information you can take in at any one moment. If you are like most people, you had no difficulty saying "3" and "5" immediately for the first two boxes, respectively, but you had to estimate for the next two boxes. If so, your attention span is about seven. In his classic 1956 paper, "The Magic Number Seven Plus or Minus Two: Some Limits on Our Capacity for Processing Information," George Miller cited evidence that when the display has less than seven dots people *subitize*—they can immediately see how many dots there are—but when the display has more than seven dots they are more likely to *estimate*. This is evidence for the idea that people have severe limits on their capacity to process information in working memory.

Let's try one more task. Read aloud each row of letters and immediately after reading the row, recite the letters aloud in order without looking at the page.

J M F

S K Y N L

N F R D M P W B T R

H C T F B R N L N Y K S M J K P X G N V

Try It!

This is called a *memory span* task because it tells how many items you can remember in a list without error. If you are like most people, you could remember the first list fine and probably the second one as well, but you made errors on the third and fourth lists. If so, your memory span is about seven. George Miller called this the *magic number 7* and also noted that when we give a list of one-syllable words the memory span is about five, and when we give a list of digits, the memory span is about nine. Again, it appears that people have a very limited working memory capacity.

Overall, George Miller was able to point out many examples showing that *short-term memory* capacity (which is similar to *working memory* capacity) is limited to about seven chunks of information, although more recent estimates have reduced that number to five. A chunk is determined by how the learner groups presented material based on the learner's prior knowledge. For example, remembering five words involves remembering 25 letters, so the word serves as a chunk. By using their prior knowledge to create larger chunks, people can effectively hold more information in working memory.

A Closer Look at Active Processing: Wittrock's Generative Processes

Please read the following paragraph, and when you are finished write a one-sentence summary in the space provided.

> To be assured her brothers would be prepared, she had prepared a message in advance. Since specific officials examined all of the slaves' mail, Harriet's message was addressed to a man named Jacob Johnson, who secretly assisted the Underground Railroad, and who was one of the relatively few free black men in Maryland. However, even Jacob's mail might be searched, so Harriet had to be cautious. Her message stated: "Inform my brothers to be always devoted to prayer, and when the sturdy aged fleet of vigor glides along to be prepared to unite aboard."

Please write your title: _____

Now please answer the following question.

> Harriet's code telling her brothers to "be prepared to unite aboard" meant
>
> a. to be aware of specific officials
> b. to get ready to escape
> c. to visit her parents
> d to contact Jacob

In a study by Marleen Doctorow, M. C. Wittrock, and Carolyn Marks, high school students were asked to read a story consisting of several paragraphs (control group) or to read the same story but write a summary sentence after reading each paragraph (as shown above). On a subsequent comprehension test consisting of questions such as shown above, students who had generated summaries scored about one standard deviation better than the control group on the comprehension test (i.e., the effect size was about $d = 1$).

M. C. Wittrock explained this finding in terms of his *generative theory of learning* in which people learn more deeply when they engage in learning strategies that prime appropriate cognitive processing during learning. For example, the *generative effect* of creating summary sentences encouraged learners to engage in cognitive processes such as organizing the material into a coherent structure and integrating the material with relevant prior knowledge.

How Learning Works:
A Cognitive Model of Learning

The *cognitive theory of multimedia learning* provides a basic description of how the human information processing system works.

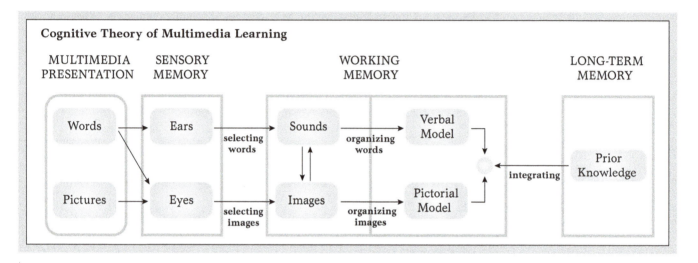

Starting on the left side of the figure (under MULTIMEDIA PRESENTATION), information is presented in words and pictures (such as a live presentation, a printed lesson in a book, or a computer-based lesson). The words can be in spoken or printed form. The pictures can be static (such as illustrations, graphs, charts, maps, or photos) or dynamic (such as animation or video). Spoken words impinge on the ears and are briefly represented as sounds in auditory sensory memory whereas printed words and pictures impinge on the eyes and are briefly represented as images in visual sensory memory (as shown under SENSORY MEMORY). If the learner attends to the fleeting sounds in sensory memory, some of the material can be transferred to WORKING MEMORY for further processing (as indicated by the "selecting words" arrow). Similarly, if the learner attends to the fleeting images, some of the material can be transferred to working memory for further processing (as indicated by the "selecting images" arrow). At this point the printed words can be converted into sounds (indicated by the arrow from "Images" to "Sounds"). Next, the learner can mentally organize the sounds in working memory to form a verbal model (as indicated by the "organizing words" arrow). Similarly, the learner can mentally organize the images in working memory to form a pictorial model (as indicated by the "organizing pictures" arrow). Finally, the learner can mentally connect the verbal and pictorial models, and can also connect them with prior knowledge that is retrieved from LONG-TERM MEMORY (as indicated by the arrow labeled "integrating"). The resulting learning outcome can then be stored in long-term memory.

Three Cognitive Science Principles in Learning

As shown in the figure, the cognitive theory of multimedia learning is consistent with three basic principles:

1. *Dual channels.* The top row ("words—ears—sounds—verbal model") represents the verbal channel, in which the learner constructs verbal representations, and the bottom row ("pictures—eyes—images—pictorial model") represents the pictorial channel, in which the learner constructs pictorial representations.
2. *Limited capacity.* The box labeled "WORKING MEMORY" can hold and process just a few selected words and images at any one time.
3. *Active processing.* The labeled arrows represent active cognitive processing, such as selecting relevant words and pictures for further processing, mentally organizing words and images into coherent representations, and integrating these verbal and pictorial representations with each other and with prior knowledge from long-term memory.

The Central Role of Prior Knowledge in Learning

As you can see in the right-most box, prior knowledge is stored in LONG-TERM MEMORY. Prior knowledge includes schemas—organizing structures for connecting knowledge elements into a coherent mental representation—which can be transferred to WORKING MEMORY (indicated by the "integrating" arrow). Working memory is limited in capacity, so only a few knowledge elements can be held at any one time.

When schemas are transferred to working memory, they can be used to help guide the process of selecting and organizing knowledge elements into coherent structures. In this process, many individual knowledge elements can be organized into a single structure, which now counts as a single knowledge element, thereby allowing more information to be held in working memory at one time. As you can see in the following table, prior knowledge plays a crucial role in learning by (a) guiding the knowledge construction process in which incoming knowledge elements are selected and organized and (b) allowing more information to be held in working memory through a process of organizing many knowledge elements into a single structure.

How Prior Knowledge Fosters Learning	
What It Does	**How It Works**
Guides knowledge construction in working memory	Schemas transferred from long-term memory provide an organizing structure for selecting and organizing incoming knowledge elements.
Allows more information in working memory	Many individual knowledge elements are organized into a single knowledge structure so more information can be processed with the same limited working memory capacity.

Three Memory Stores in Meaningful Learning

As you can see in the figure, the three memory stores are represented as rectangles:

1. *Sensory memory* holds information in the same sensory format as presented, has large capacity, and lasts for a very brief time (less that a quarter of a second). Spoken words impinging in the ears are held briefly as sounds in auditory sensory memory and printed words and pictures impinging on the eyes are held briefly as images in visual sensory memory.
2. *Working memory* holds information in an organized format, has limited capacity, and lasts for a short time (less than half of a minute) unless actively processed.
3. *Long-term memory* holds information in an organized format, has large capacity, and lasts for long periods of time (many years).

Three Memory Stores Involved in Meaningful Learning

Memory Store	Format	Duration	Capacity
Sensory memory	Sensory	Very brief	Large
Working memory	Organized	Short	Small
Long-term memory	Organized	Long	Large

The architecture of the human information processing system has implications for learning. In terms of capacity, working memory is a bottleneck in the system because working memory has limited capacity whereas the other stores have large capacity. To compensate, learners must be careful to select relevant information for further processing and must mentally organize the material into a coherent representation that requires less capacity to hold, often using existing knowledge structures (called *schemas*) to help structure incoming material. Thus, we are designed to be sense makers.

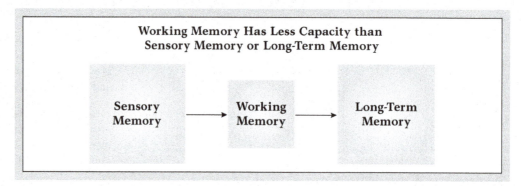

Working Memory Has Less Capacity than Sensory Memory or Long-Term Memory

Sensory Memory → Working Memory → Long-Term Memory

Three Cognitive Processes in Meaningful Learning

As you can also see in the "Cognitive Theory of Multimedia" figure, there are three kinds of cognitive processes:

1. *Selecting* is paying attention to relevant portions of incoming words and pictures.
2. *Organizing* is mentally organizing the selected words into a coherent verbal model and mentally organizing the selected images into a coherent pictorial mode.
3. *Integrating* is making connections between representations in working memory and with prior knowledge from long-term memory.

Three Cognitive Processes Required for Meaningful Learning

Process	Description	Location
Selecting	Paying attention to relevant words and pictures	Transfer information from sensory memory to working memory
Organizing	Organizing selected words and pictures into coherent mental representations	Manipulate information in working memory
Integrating	Connecting verbal and pictorial representations with each other and with prior knowledge	Transfer knowledge from long-term memory to working memory

The cognitive processes are what make learning happen in the human information system. For meaningful learning to occur, learners must engage in all three kinds of cognitive processing—selecting, organizing, and integrating—represented by the three labeled arrows in the next figure. *Active learning* refers to engaging in these cognitive processes during learning. The arrow from working memory to long-term memory represents the process of encoding.

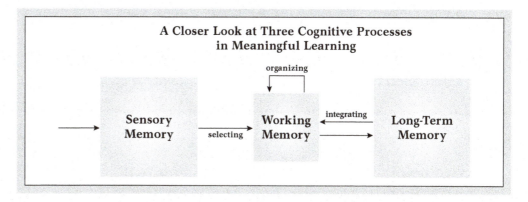

A Closer Look at Three Cognitive Processes in Meaningful Learning

The Mighty Ms:
Motivation and Metacognition

What is missing from our explanation of how learning works? As you can see in the flowchart shown in the figure on this page, the processing tends to go mainly from left to right (i.e., from outside to inside)—when material comes in from the outside world we select relevant information, organize it into a coherent representation, and integrate it with prior knowledge. What instigates and maintains all this cognitive processing? What guides all this cognitive processing? How do know what to do?

What is missing from the flowchart is an account of how the learner knows when to use appropriate learning processes (which can be called *metacognition*) and why the learner wants to use them (which can be called *motivation*). The learner's contribution to the learning process is indicated by adding new arrows along the bottom of the flowchart from the learner's long-term memory back to the cognitive processes of selecting, organizing, and integrating. The added arrows go from right to left (i.e., from inside to outside), thus complementing the cognitive theory of multimedia learning described in the previous section (pp. 34–37). The added arrows are intended to recognize the role of motivation and metacognition in learning, but much more work is needed to explicate how they work. In the following sections, we briefly explore the role of what I nickname as the *mighty Ms* of motivation and metacognition.

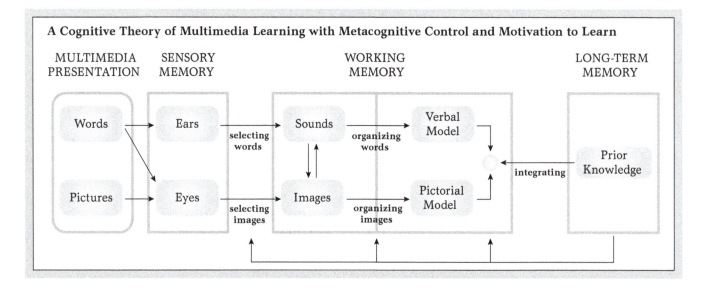

A Cognitive Theory of Multimedia Learning with Metacognitive Control and Motivation to Learn

Motivation to Learn

What Is the Role of Academic Motivation in Learning?

Consider a classroom where an instructor presents a well-designed lesson on how to compute statistical tests. Avery works hard to understand the material—by taking notes, asking questions about elements that do not make sense to her, and trying practice problems until she can get them right—whereas Beth does not work hard to understand the material—by barely paying attention to the lesson. In these scenarios, we can say that Avery is motivated to learn whereas Beth is not motivated to learn.

Motivation to learn (or what can be called *academic motivation*) is reflected in the amount of effort a student exerts to make sense of the material—that is, to engage in the appropriate cognitive processes of selecting, organizing, and integrating (shown in the figure on the left). Meaningful learning cannot occur if students do not exert effort to engage in appropriate cognitive processing during learning. For this reason, motivation to learn (or simply *motivation*) is a prerequisite for meaningful learning.

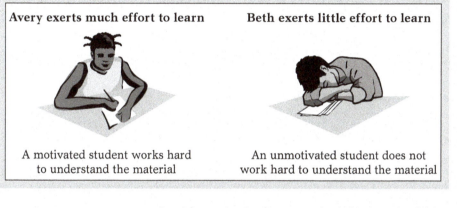

Avery exerts much effort to learn

A motivated student works hard to understand the material

Beth exerts little effort to learn

An unmotivated student does not work hard to understand the material

What Is Motivation?

Motivation is an internal state that initiates and maintains goal directed behavior. This definition has four components—motivation is personal, activating, energizing, and directed—as shown in the following table.

The Four Components of Motivation		
Component	**Description**	**Part of Definition**
personal	Occurs within the student	Motivation is an internal state
activating	instigates behavior	that initiates
energizing	fosters persistence and intensity	and maintains
directed	aimed at accomplishing a goal	goal-directed behavior.

In the context of learning environments, motivation instigates and maintains the learner's efforts to engage in the cognitive processes required for making sense of the to-be-learned material.

How Motivation Works

Five Conceptions of How Motivation Works

Let me ask you to rate a few statements about how you see yourself as a learner. For each statement circle the number that best corresponds to your level of agreement (with 1 as "strongly disagree" and 7 as "strongly agree"). Don't worry, I can't see what you circle.

A Learning Questionnaire

I am interested in learning about how learning works.

DISAGREE   1   2   3   4   5   6   7   AGREE

I am good at learning the kind of material in this book.

DISAGREE   1   2   3   4   5   6   7   AGREE

If I perform poorly on a section quiz, it is because I did not try hard enough to learn.

DISAGREE   1   2   3   4   5   6   7   AGREE

In reading this book, my goal is to perform better than others on a quiz.

DISAGREE   1   2   3   4   5   6   7   AGREE

In reading this book, I feel as if the author is working with me.

DISAGREE   1   2   3   4   5   6   7   AGREE

Each of these statements reflects a conception of how academic motivation works. The first one is an example of motivation based on your interest, the second one reflects motivation based on your self-efficacy beliefs, the third one taps your motivation based on your attributions, the fourth is concerned with your motivation based on your goal orientation, and the last one seeks to evaluate your motivation based on your sense of social partnership. Among cognitive theories of motivation, the five most popular conceptions of how academic motivation works are:

1. *Motivation based on interest*: The idea that students work harder to learn when the to-be-learned material has personal value or interest for them. For example, students will work harder to understand a statistics lesson if they like statistics and see that the topic has value to them in support of career objectives or personal interest.
2. *Motivation based on beliefs*: The idea that students work harder to learn when they believe their hard work will pay off. Students with high *self-efficacy beliefs* have the belief that they are capable of doing well on a particular learning task, such as learning statistics, and therefore exert more effort to learn.
3. *Motivation based on attributions*: The idea that students work harder to learn when they attribute their academic successes and failures to their effort during learning rather than to their ability or other factors. Students who make *effort-based attributions* (interpreting their academic successes and failures as caused by their own level of ef-

fort during learning) are more likely to exert effort during learning when they want to succeed.

4. *Motivation based on goals*: The idea that students work harder to learn when their academic goal is to perform well (*performance-approach goal*) or to master the material (*mastery goal*) rather than to avoid performing poorly (*performance-avoidance goal*). In short, students' academic goals affect how much effort they put into learning.

5. *Motivation based on social partnership*: The idea that students work harder to learn when they view the instructor as a social partner who is trying to work together with them. According to *social agency theory*, social cues such as the instructor using conversational style rather than formal style or providing self-revealing comments, can help create a sense of social partnership in which the learner feels part of a learning team.

Five Conceptions of How Motivation Works		
Basis	**Description**	**Example**
Interest	Students work harder to learn material that has personal value to them.	I like this.
Beliefs	Students work harder to learn when they believe their hard work will pay off.	I am good at this.
Attributions	Students work harder to learn when they attribute their successes and failures to effort.	My success or failure on this depends on my effort.
Goals	Students work harder to learn when their goal is to master the material.	I want to learn this.
Partnership	Students work harder to learn when they view the instructor as a social partner.	We are working together to learn this.

As you can see these five conceptualizations are not mutually exclusive—that is, if one is right that does not mean that the others are wrong. In fact, research on motivation includes evidence to support each of these conceptions of motivation.

Classic theories of motivation are derived largely from animal research, often with hungry rats, and conceptualize motivation as based on drive reduction—that is, we do things to satisfy biological needs such as the need for food, drink, exploration, and so on. In contrast, modern theories of academic motivation—that is, what motivates students to work hard to learn in school—are derived largely from human research, often in school settings, and conceptualize motivation as based on the learner's cognitions—such as shown in the preceding table. Any complete account of how learning works must include the role of the learner's motivation to learn.

Metacognition in Learning

Do you have a good idea of how you learn—such as how you learn from this book? To help answer that question, please respond to each statement in the following questionnaire.

A Learning Questionnaire

Please place a check mark in the space that best applies to you for each statement.

1. When reading this book, I try to relate the material to what I already know.

   ___ Never   ___ Rarely   ___ Sometimes   ___ Often   ___ Always

2. When I become confused about something I'm reading in this book, I go back and try to figure it out.

   ___ Never   ___ Rarely   ___ Sometimes   ___ Often   ___ Always

3. Before I study a new section of this book thoroughly, I often skim it to see how well it is organized.

   ___ Never   ___ Rarely   ___ Sometimes   ___ Often   ___ Always

4. Whenever I read an assertion or conclusion in this book, I think about possible alternatives.

   ___ Never   ___ Rarely   ___ Sometimes   ___ Often   ___ Always

---

This little exercise gives you an example of the types of items you might find on a questionnaire aimed at assessing your metacognition—that is, how well you know how you learn and how well you control your learning process. In particular, these items are adapted from a longer questionnaire—the Motivated Learning Strategies Questionnaire (MLSQ)— developed by Paul Pintrich and Dale Schunk.

What Is the Relation between Metacognition and Motivation?

Metacognitive strategies refer to a person's knowledge about how to improve his or her learning. Yet, having metacognitive knowledge is just half the story; you must also be motivated to use the metacognitive strategies appropriately in the course of learning. That is, even if you know how to help yourself learn, you have to want to exert the effort needed to learn.

What Is Metacognition?

Metacognition refers to awareness of one's cognitive processing and control of one's cognitive processing. When we focus specifically on learning, metacognition refers to the learners' knowledge of how they learn (i.e., cognitive processing during learning) and the learners' control of the learning process (i.e., control of cognitive processing). As shown in the following table, this definition has two components—metacognitive awareness and metacognitive control.

Two Components of Metacognition

Component	Definition	Example
Awareness	Knowing how one learns	I know that paraphrasing helps me learn a complicated idea.
Control	Knowing how to monitor and control one's learning	I notice that I am having trouble making sense of this definition, so I rewrite it in my own words.

What Is Comprehension Monitoring?

Comprehension monitoring is awareness of how well you understand what you are reading. Please read the following passage (used in research by Ellen Markman) and let me know if everything makes sense to you.

A Fish Story

Many different kinds of fish live in the ocean. Some fish live near the surface of the water, but some live all the way down at the bottom of the ocean. There is absolutely no light at the bottom of the ocean. Some fish that live at the bottom of the ocean know their food by its color. They will eat only red fungus.

Almost all of the elementary school children in Ellen Markman's study did not recognize the inconsistency between having no light at the bottom of the ocean and fish being able to see color at the bottom of the ocean. Recognizing inconsistencies in what you are reading is an indication that you are engaging in comprehension monitoring. This example shows that comprehension monitoring is a specific type of metacognition—and one that develops as learners gain more experience in academic reading.

What Is the Role of Metacognition in Learning?

Metacognition plays a central role in learning, by helping to guide the learner's cognitive processing of the to-be-learned material. *Self-regulated learners* have both metacognitive awareness—they know learning strategies that work for them—and metacognitive control—they are able to recognize when it is appropriate to use them during learning. Thus, self-regulated learners understand how they learn and take responsibility for monitoring and controlling their learning. A major goal of education is to help people become self-regulated learners. Any complete account of how learning works must include the role of the learner's metacognitive processing during learning.

Learning in Subject Areas

In attempting to build a theory of learning, researchers have taken three approaches to the breadth of learning theory—general theories, mini-models, and psychology of subject areas.

How Broad Should Learning Theory Be?		
Approach	**Applications**	**Typical Venues**
General theory	All situations	Rats learn to run a maze, or humans memorize word lists
Mini-models	Small tasks	People learn to solve a given type of puzzle
Psychology of subject areas	School subjects	People learn to read, write, or solve arithmetic problems

General Theory of Learning

For most of its early history, the science of learning sought to establish a general theory of learning—that is, a theory of learning applicable across all learning situations. An example of an attempt to build a general theory of learning is Thorndike's law of effect (as described on pages 24–25). Surprisingly, the search for a general theory of learning was mainly based on artificial laboratory tasks—such as how a hungry rat learned to run a maze or how humans memorized word lists. By the mid-1900s it had become clear that the science of learning had fostered so many competing general theories of learning that it was not able to reach consensus on a unified theory of how learning works. In short, the search for a general theory of learning was too broad.

Mini-Models of Learning

As a reaction, researchers gave up on general principles of learning and sought instead to describe learning and cognitive processing in specific laboratory tasks. For example, in a linear order task, people may be asked to judge, "If Tom is taller than Pete, and Pete is taller than Jake, then is Tom taller than Jake?" Most mini-models continued in the tradition of using artificial laboratory tasks but focused on humans rather than lab animals. By the 1980s, it had become clear that a collection of mini-models is not the same as a theory of learning. In short, the search for mini-models was too narrow.

Psychology of Subject Areas

Something exciting happened next that has changed the science of learning. Just as the science of learning was about to collapse of its own failure to find a general theory of learning or its boredom in creating mini-theories of small artificial tasks, researchers became interested in studying learning in more authentic situations, including educationally relevant situations. One of the resulting success stories involved applying the science of learning to the study of how people learn school subjects, such as how to read, how to write, or how to do arithmetic. In short, the psychologies of subject areas approach has turned out to be just right.

Although a review of research on learning in school subjects is beyond our scope in this book, the following table lists example tasks and exemplary findings for the school subjects of reading, writing, mathematics, science, and history.

Advances in the Psychology of Subject Areas

Topic	Example Task	Exemplary Finding
Reading fluency	Say a printed word aloud.	Phonological awareness (ability to hear and produce the sounds in one's language) is a prerequisite for learning to read words.
Reading comprehension	Summarize the point of a printed text.	The learner's prior knowledge affects what they learn from a printed text.
Writing	Produce an essay on a given topic.	Successful writers tend to engage in planning before they start to write.
Mathematics	Solve a word problem.	Number sense (such as the concept of a mental number line) is a prerequisite for solving arithmetic problems.
Science	Predict what will happen in an experiment.	Learning can involve conceptual change (in which the learners find that their existing conception conflicts with their observations).
History	Critique an argument.	Experts are more likely to consider the credibility of sources of information.

In my book *Learning and Instruction*, I have shown that advances in our understanding of how people learn in key subject areas have useful implications for how to improve instruction. Here is how I described psychologies of subject areas:

What Are Psychologies of Subject Areas?

In contrast to traditional experimental psychology's focus on general theories of how people learn or develop or think, today's educational psychology seeks to build domain-specific theories within each subject area. For example, instead of asking domain-general questions such as, "How do people learn?" "How do people develop?" or "How do people think?" we can ask, "How do people learn to solve mathematics problems?" "How do people develop mathematical competence?" or "How do people think mathematically?" By examining cognition in the context of real academic tasks rather than in contrived laboratory tasks, we can develop more realistic theories of how people learn, develop, and think. (pp. 31–32)

Psychologies of subject areas extend to training of adults in job-related competencies ranging from how to be an effective leader to how to troubleshoot computer problems to how to be an instructional designer. Similarly, this approach applies to professional training in areas ranging from medicine to law to business.

Eight Things We Know about Learning from Word Lists

Since the late 1800s psychologists have been carefully studying how people learn a list of words. In *free recall list learning*, the learner may see one word every second and then be asked to recall the words in any order. In *serial list learning*, the learner may see one word every second and then be asked to recall them in order. In *paired-associate learning*, the learner may see a series of word pairs to study and then be given the first word in each pair and asked to recall the second word.

Three Kinds of List Learning		
Type	**Description**	**Example**
Free recall list learning	Receive one word at a time; recall words in any order.	Learn the 50 states in the United States.
Serial list learning	Receive one word at a time; recall them in order of presentation.	Memorize the alphabet or days of the week.
Paired-associate learning	Receive one word pair at a time; recall second word in each pair when cued with first word.	Learn the corresponding word in Spanish for each of 10 English words.

The table on the right lists eight major learning effects that are based on studying how people learn a list of words (and indicates in brackets the corresponding page in the book where the effect is examined, if applicable). I have selected effects that are relevant to practical learning tasks. As you can see, the first two findings are the learning curve and the forgetting curve, respectively—two persistent findings that apply across many different learning situations. Learning requires effort and needs periodic renewed effort.

The next two findings refer to the characteristics of the human learning system—it has separate channels for words and pictures (which I call the *dual channel principle*) and the channels are limited in processing capacity (which I call the *limited capacity principle*).

Finally, each of the next four findings relates to aspects of the third characteristic of the human learning system—it requires appropriate cognitive processing during learning. These findings demonstrate that learning can involve mentally organizing the incoming material and assimilating it to existing knowledge—that is, learning is a sort of sense making activity rather than a process of simply adding information to memory.

Why do I include a section on list learning in a book intended to focus on meaningful learning? A pervasive finding from decades of research on word lists is that even in this somewhat sterile learning environment, learners exhibit ways to engage in sense making. We examine the instructional implications of these basic learning findings in the next section of the book.

Eight Things We Know About Learning Word Lists

Finding	Description: What Is It?	Implications: What's the Big Idea?
Learning curve [p. 26]	The more you study a list of words, the more you learn.	Learning outcomes depend on time on task.
Forgetting curve [p. 27]	The longer you wait after learning a list of words, the less you remember.	Forgetting depends on time since learning.
Concreteness effect [p. 31]	Concrete words are easier to remember than abstract words.	Learning takes place in a cognitive system that has separate channels for words and pictures.
Memory span effect [p. 32]	The longest list of words people can recall after one presentation contains fewer than 7 words.	Learning takes place in a cognitive system that is limited in processing capacity.
Clustering in free recall	You tend to recall the words in a list by category (i.e., furniture, parts of the body, professions, etc.) in spite of the presentation order.	Organizational processes during learning affect learning.
Release from proactive interference	Your memory declines for a word list that contains words from the same category, but recovers when you switch to a list of words from a new category.	Learning can involve assimilating new material to existing knowledge.
State-dependent learning	You remember a word list better if the testing situation is similar to the learning situation.	Learning is situated in specific contexts.
Levels of processing	If you engage in deep processing of words during learning, you remember more.	Generative processes during learning affect learning.

References and Suggested Readings

Pages 14–17

Bransford, J. D., Brown, A. L., & Cocking, R. R. (Eds.). (1999). *How people learn*. Washington, DC: National Academy Press.

A summary of research evidence on how people learn, commissioned by the National Research Council and written by a team of prominent researchers.

Mayer, R. E. (2008). *Learning and instruction* (2nd ed.). Upper Saddle River, NJ: Pearson/Merrill Prentice Hall.

An up-to-date summary of research on learning in subject areas such as reading, writing, mathematics, and science.

Pages 18–19

Shavelson, R. J., & Towne, L. (Eds.). (2002). *Scientific research in education*. Washington, DC: National Academy Press.

A consensus document summarizing six principles for conducting scientific research in education.

Pages 20–21

Pressley, M., & Woloshyn, V. (1995). *Cognitive strategy instruction that really improves children's academic performance*. Cambridge, MA: Brookline Books.

A review of research on strategy training.

Thorndike, E. L., & Woodworth, R. S. (1901). The influence of improvement in one mental function upon the efficiency of other mental functions. *Psychological Review, 8,* 247–261.

A classic research study on transfer of learning.

Pages 22–29

Bartlett, F. C. (1932). *Remembering*. London: Cambridge University Press.

A classic book in the science of learning describing important research on meaningful learning.

Ebbinghaus, H. (1964). *Memory*. New York: Dover. [Originally published in German in 1885.]

A classic book in the science of learning describing the world's first experiments on learning.

Thorndike, E. L. (1911). *Animal learning*. New York: Macmillan.

A classic book in the science of learning by the world's first educational psychologist.

Pages 30–33

Doctorow, M., Wittrock, M. C., & Marks, C. (1978). Generative processes in reading comprehension. *Journal of Educational Psychology, 70,* 109–118.

A landmark paper providing evidence for Wittrock's generative theory of learning.

Miller, G. (1956). The magic number seven, plus or minus two: Some limits on our capacity for processing information. *Psychological Review, 63,* 81–97.

A landmark paper heralding the beginning of the cognitive revolution in the science of learning.

Paivio, A. (1971). *Imagery and verbal processes*. New York: Holt, Rinehart and Winston.

A classic book in the science of learning that spotlights the distinction between pictorial representations and verbal representations.

Wittrock, M. C. (1989). Generative processes in comprehension. *Educational Psychologist, 24,* 345–376.

A statement of Wittrock's theory of generative learning.

Pages 34–37

Mayer, R. E. (2009). *Multimedia learning* (2nd ed.). New York: Cambridge University Press.

Describes how learning works based on a cognitive theory of multimedia learning.

Pages 38–43

Markman, E. (1979). Realizing that you don't understand: Elementary school children's awareness of inconsistencies. *Child Development, 50,* 643–655.

McCormick, C. B. (2003). Metacognition and learning. In W. M. Reynolds & G. E. Miller (Eds.), *Handbook of psychology* (vol. 7; pp. 79–102). New York: Wiley.

An overview of research and theory on metacognition in academic learning.

Moreno, R., & Mayer, R. E. (2006). Interactive multimodal learning environments. *Educational Psychology Review, 19,* 309–326.

Presents a cognitive-affective model of learning with media, which includes arrows representing the role of motivation and metacognition.

Pintrich, P. R., & Schunk, D. H. (2002). *Motivation in education.* Upper Saddle River, NJ: Pearson/Merrill Prentice Hall.

A review of research and theory on academic motivation.

Pages 44–45

Mayer, R. E. (2008). *Learning and instruction* (2nd ed.). Upper Saddle River, NJ: Pearson/Merrill Prentice Hall.

An up-to-date summary of research on learning in subject areas such as reading, writing, mathematics, and science.

Pages 46–47

Tarpy, R., & Mayer, R. E. (1978). *Foundations of learning and memory.* Glenview, IL: Scott, Foresman & Co.

A survey of classic research on learning.

How Instruction Works

Once we understand how learning works in educational contexts, the next step in applying the science of learning is to create instruction that promotes intended learning outcomes. Instruction is the instructor's attempt to promote a change in the knowledge of the learner. The science of instruction is concerned with identifying instructional methods that are suggested by the science of learning, and determining whether, when, and how they work.

When you are considering which instructional method to use, it is appropriate to ask what works, when it works, and how it works. These are the issues addressed in the science of instruction.

In this section, I provide a brief overview of how instruction works by exploring each of the subtopics listed below.

Bite-Size Chunks of the Science of Instruction

What Is Instruction?

What Is the Science of Instruction?

What Is an Instructional Objective?

    Three Levels of Instructional Objectives

    Five Kinds of Knowledge in Instructional Objectives

    Six Kinds of Cognitive Processes in Instructional Objectives

How Instruction Works: Three Demands on Cognitive Capacity

How Instruction Works: Three Instructional Scenarios

Twelve Instructional Design Principles for Lesson Learning

    Evidence-Based Instructional Principles for Reducing Extraneous Processing

    Evidence-Based Instructional Principles for Managing Essential Processing

    Evidence-Based Instructional Principles for Fostering Generative Processing

Eight Instructional Design Principles for Effective Studying

    Evidence-Based Principles for Studying by Practicing

    Evidence-Based Principles for Studying by Generating

How to Guide Cognitive Processing during Learning

    Instructional Techniques for Selecting

    Instructional Techniques for Organizing

    Instructional Techniques for Integrating

Three Popular but Questionable Principles

A Closer Look at Active Teaching and Learning

What Is Instruction?

Instruction is the instructor's manipulation of the learner's environment in order to foster learning. This definition has two parts—instruction is something the instructor does and the intention of the instructor is to help someone learn something.

Let's examine the two parts in more detail. First, instruction is a manipulation of the environment. This manipulation can be something as simple as having a lecturer smile and gesture as she delivers a lecture. The manipulation of the learner's environment is called the *instructional method* (or *instructional treatment*).

Second, the manipulation is intended to cause a change in the learner's knowledge. When we say that an instructional method or treatment is effective, we mean that it caused the intended change in the learner's knowledge.

Instruction is the instructor's manipulation of the learner's environment in order to foster learning.

Instruction is

1. manipulating what the learner experiences
2. with the intention to cause a change in the learner's knowledge.

The figure on the right shows the relations among instruction, learning, and assessment. The goal of instruction is to create an environment that causes an experience for the learner that in turn leads to knowledge change (represented by the arrow from "manipulation" to "experience" and the arrow from "experience" to "knowledge"). Learning is the change in knowledge attributable to the learner's experience (represented by the arrow from "experience" to "knowledge"). In short, it is not possible to talk about instruction without talking about learning, because learning is part of the goal of instruction. The last step in the figure involves assessing what was learned, which is a necessary step in determining the effectiveness of an instructional manipulation. We infer a change in the learner's knowledge by detecting a change in the learner's performance (represented by the arrow from "knowledge" to "performance").

As you can see, there are two characters in the instructional episode—the instructor and the learner. The instructor's role is to create an environment that causes the learner to have experiences that lead to the intended knowledge change (indicated by "What the instructor does"). The learner's role is to interact with the environment in ways that create experiences that lead to the intended knowledge change (indicated by "What goes on inside the learner's mind"). We can determine what learning has occurred by observing the learner's performance on a test (indicated by "What the learner does"). In short, the instructor creates the learning environment and the learner experiences the learning environment that the instructor has created.

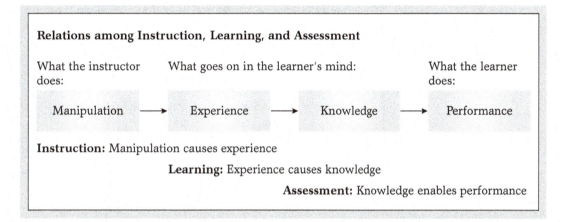

Relations among Instruction, Learning, and Assessment

What the instructor does: / What goes on in the learner's mind: / What the learner does:

Manipulation → Experience → Knowledge → Performance

Instruction: Manipulation causes experience

Learning: Experience causes knowledge

Assessment: Knowledge enables performance

In sum, instruction occurs when a manipulation of the learner's environment causes experience in the learner, which in turn causes knowledge change in the learner; learning occurs when experience causes knowledge change in the learner; and assessment occurs when the learner's knowledge enables performance that can be detected in an assessment.

What Is the Science of Instruction?

We defined the science of instruction in the introduction, but let's elaborate a bit on that definition.

What is the science of instruction?

Definition:	The science of instruction is the scientific study of how to help people learn.
Goal:	Research-based principles of instructional design indicating which instructional methods work for teaching which kinds of knowledge to which kinds of learners under which kinds of circumstances.
Criterion:	Instructional methods are based on evidence.

The science of instruction is the scientific study of how to help people learn. What makes it scientific is that instructional principles are tested in research studies rather than being based on fads, ideology, or common practice.

The goal of the science of instruction is to determine research-based principles for how to design effective instruction. For each principle, there are likely to be boundary conditions under which the principle is most effective—such as for certain kinds of learners, certain kinds of knowledge, and certain circumstances.

The main criterion for using an instructional method is whether there is convincing evidence of its effectiveness. The primary means of testing whether an instructional method causes learning is to conduct experiments comparing the *learning outcomes* (e.g., test performance) of people who were taught with or without a particular instructional method.

What Is Evidence-Based Practice?

The science of instruction seeks to support *evidence-based practice*—instructional practices that are supported by rigorous research findings. Here is how Richard Shavelson and Lisa Towne make the case for evidence-based practice in their National Research Council report, *Scientific Research in Education:*

The Case for Evidence-Based Practice

No one would think of going to the Moon or wiping out a disease without research. Likewise, one cannot expect reform efforts in education to have significant effects without research-based knowledge to guide them. (p. 1)

Educational decisions are not always based on research evidence. In *Scientific Research in Education,* Richard Shavelson and Lisa Towne note that educational decisions are sometimes based on ideology or opinion:

Alternatives to Evidence-Based Practice

Decisions about education are sometimes instituted with no scientific basis at all, but rather are derived from ideology or deeply held beliefs. (p. 17)

Let's consider three approaches to making decisions about educational practice—ideological, common practice, and evidence-based approaches. In an ideological approach, decisions are based on ideologies—overarching theories that are not scientifically tested—such as the radical social constructivist view (often attributed to the famous Russian psychologist, Lev Vygotsky) that deep learning only takes place in groups through peer discussion. In the common-practice approach, decisions are consistent with commonly used methods that often are touted by opinion leaders in the field—such as the "best practice" of arranging students into groups of four to work together on solving mathematics problems. What is wrong with ideology or common practice as the basis for educational decisions? The problem is that such approaches often conflict with rigorous research evidence, such as the large body of research evidence summarized by Robert Slavin and colleagues in the *Handbook of Psychology* showing that group learning with a single group reward generally is ineffective.

Three Approaches to Instructional Practice	
Approach	**Example Involving Collaborative Groups**
Ideological approach	Vygotsky says that learning occurs in a social context through peer discussion.
Common-practice approach	Opinion leaders in mathematics education point to the ubiquitous use of collaborative groups.
Evidence-based approach	Research shows that students who work in groups do not learn better if they are given rewards based on group performance.

What Is an Instructional Objective?

An instructional objective specifies an intended change in the learner's knowledge. An instructional objective answers the question: What is the learner supposed to know after instruction that he or she did not know before instruction? A complete instructional objective has three parts:

1. *What you learned.* It specifies the knowledge that is learned.
2. *How you use it.* It specifies what the learner does with the knowledge in performing a task.
3. *How we interpret your performance.* It describes how to interpret the learner's performance.

In *Knowing What Students Know: The Science and Design of Educational Assessment,* James Pellegrino, Naomi Chudowsky, and Robert Glaser refer to these three elements as the achievement that is to be assessed, tasks used to collect evidence about student achievement, and methods used to interpret the resulting evidence, respectively. In many cases, the third element is only implied—that is, that the learner is successful on the target task. Instructional objectives are stated in the future tense as a goal—describing what will be learned—whereas assessment works in the past tense—describing what was learned.

What Is an Instructional Objective?

An instructional objective specifies an intended change in the learner's knowledge. It includes a description of (1) what was learned, (2) how it is used, and (3) how to interpret the learner's performance.

Consider an instructional objective: "The student will be able to solve two-column multiplication problems." In this case, the three parts can be characterized as follows:

1. What you learn is the procedure for two-column multiplication.
2. How you use it is to solve multiplication problems such as $35 \times 57 =$ ___.
3. How we interpret your performance is implied to be a tally of the percentage of correct answers on a set of problems.

According to classic definitions such as proposed by Robert Mager in his famous book *Preparing Instructional Objectives,* an instructional objective should state (1) the *task* to be performed, (2) the *conditions* under which it will performed, and (3) the *criteria* by which performance will be evaluated—paralleling the three elements in the preceding box.

Distinction between Cognition and Performance

Our definition of instructional objective involves a distinction between learning and performance. Learning refers to the change in knowledge whereas performance refers to the learner's performance on a task in which the knowledge is used. Based on performance, we can infer that there was a change in the learner's knowledge.

Limitations

As you can see, the definition of instructional objective is limited to cognitive changes, that is, changes in knowledge. However, I use knowledge in the broadest sense to include beliefs (which are related to feelings), social knowledge (which guides performance on social tasks), and motor knowledge (which guides performance on physical tasks).

Three Levels of Instructional Objectives

In *A Taxonomy for Learning, Teaching, and Assessing: A Revision of Bloom's Taxonomy of Educational Objectives,* Lorin Anderson and colleagues distinguished among three levels of objectives:

1. *Global objectives* are general statements intended to provide vision for educators
2. *Educational objectives* are moderately specific statements intended to guide curriculum development
3. *Instructional objectives* are specific statements intended to guide preparation of lessons or lesson segments

The following table summarizes the three levels of objectives and provides examples of each.

Three Levels of Objectives			
Level	**Breadth**	**Purpose**	**Examples**
Global	General	Provide vision	All students will start school ready to learn.
			All students will learn to use their mind well, so they will be prepared for responsible citizenship, further learning, and productive employment in our nation's economy.
Educational	Moderate	Design curriculum	Ability to read musical scores.
			Ability to interpret various types of graphs.
Instructional	Specific	Prepare lesson	The student will be able to solve two-column multiplication problems.
			The student is able to classify objectives as global, educational, or instructional.

Now let's see how well you have mastered the instructional objective of this lesson. Please place a check mark next to the item(s) that fit the definition of instructional objective.

Check the instructional objective(s):

____ All students will be exposed to computer-based technology for at least 30 minutes per week

____ Understands technology's role in society

____ Ability to use educational software

____ Ability to create a PowerPoint presentation that includes graphics, text, and audio

---

If you checked only the fourth box, you are indicating that you learned how to classify objectives. The first statement is not an objective at all because it describes an activity we want the student to do rather than a change in the learner's knowledge. It is certainly appropriate for educational leaders to manage how time is allocated to various subject areas, but this is not the same as specifying instructional objectives. The second statement is a global objective and the third statement is an educational objective. Both are not specific enough to count as instructional objectives. However, sometimes standards, frameworks, and grade-level expectations are stated at the global or educational level, rendering them difficult to implement in lessons.

In this book, I focus primarily on instructional objectives, because they specify the desired change in the learner's knowledge.

Five Kinds of Knowledge
in Instructional Objectives

The first element in an instructional objective is to specify a change in knowledge. Knowledge is at the heart of learning, instruction, and assessment. Thus, it is worthwhile to distinguish among some types of knowledge that are most relevant to academic learning. The following table distinguishes among five qualitatively different kinds of knowledge—*factual knowledge, conceptual knowledge, procedural knowledge, strategic knowledge,* and *belief-based knowledge.*

Five Kinds of Knowledge		
Type	**Definition**	**Example**
Facts	Factual knowledge about the world	Boston is in Massachusetts.
Concepts	Categories, schemas, models, or principles	In the number 65, 6 refers to the number of tens.
Procedures	A step-by-step process	Multiplication of 252 × 12.
Strategies	A general method	Breaking a problem into parts.
Beliefs	Thoughts about learning	Thinking "I am not good at statistics."

For success on many academic tasks, learners need to possess all five kinds of knowledge. For example, to solve an arithmetic word problem, a learner needs to know facts (such as "There are 100 pennies in a dollar"), concepts (such as categories for word, mixture, and time-rate-distance problems), procedures (such as being able to carry out basic arithmetic), strategies (such as being able to develop a solution plan based on breaking a problem into parts), and beliefs (such as thinking "I am good at this").

The fourth category, labeled "Strategies," includes *meta-strategies,* which are strategies for managing strategies (and other knowledge). Meta-strategies are used for judging whether a particular solution plan is working or whether a particular strategy is appropriate for a given task. In some cases, affective evaluations (or *attitudes*) about elements of learning (such as "I don't like statistics") can be included in the fifth category.

An instructional objective involves a change in one (or more) of these five kinds of knowledge. In classic approaches, the learner's competencies can be broken into knowledge (corresponding to facts and concepts), skills (corresponding to procedures and strategies), and attitudes (corresponding to beliefs). As you can see, I am using knowledge in the broad sense to refer to what the learner knows. In addition, the learner may have episodic knowledge (i.e., knowledge of personal experience), which is normally not the primary goal of academic learning.

Six Kinds of Cognitive Processes in Instructional Objectives

The second step in an instructional objective is to specify how the knowledge will be used. The following table distinguishes among six kinds of cognitive processes that can be applied to the learner's knowledge. It is based on a revision of Bloom's taxonomy of educational objectives—a well-known analysis of the types of instructional objectives.

Six Kinds of Cognitive Processes		
Process	**Definition**	**Example**
Remember	Retrieve relevant knowledge from long-term memory.	State the formula for binomial probability.
Understand	Construct meaning from instructional messages.	Restate the formula for binomial probability in your own words.
Apply	Carry out or use a procedure in a given situation.	Compute the value of binomial probability given values for N, r, and p.
Analyze	Break material into its constituent parts and determine how the parts relate to one another and to an overall structure or purpose.	Distinguish between relevant and irrelevant numbers in a probability word problem.
Evaluate	Make judgments based on criteria or standards.	Judge which of two methods is the best way to solve a probability word problem.
Create	Put elements together to form a coherent or functional whole; reorganize elements into a new pattern or structure.	Plan an essay on the discovery of binomial probability.

As you can see, the kind of cognitive process(es) required depends on the task in which the knowledge will be used. For example, remembering a formula is different than using it to compute an answer, which is different from evaluating whether it was used correctly. An instructional objective involves one of the six kinds of cognitive processes applied to one of the five kinds of knowledge.

How Instruction Works:
Three Demands on Cognitive Capacity

The goal of instruction is to help the learner achieve the learning objective. Specifically, the goal of instruction is to help the learner construct the intended knowledge by guiding the learner's cognitive processing during learning. This processing must take place within the learner's cognitive system, which has limited capacity for cognitive processing. The major challenge of instructional design is to ensure that the learner engages in appropriate cognitive processing during learning while not overloading the learner's capacity for this processing. In short, instructional designers have two competing goals: (1) to encourage appropriate cognitive processing during learning and (2) to not overload the learner's cognitive system.

The following box lists three major processing demands on the learner's cognitive system during learning—*extraneous processing, essential processing,* and *generative processing.*

Three Demands on Cognitive Capacity

Extraneous processing

Definition:	Cognitive processing during learning that does not support the objective of the lesson.
Cause:	Caused by poor instructional design (or poor learner strategies).
Example:	Learners scan back and forth between text on one page and a corresponding graphic on another page.

Essential processing

Definition:	Basic cognitive processing during learning required to mentally represent the presented material (such as selecting and initial organizing).
Cause:	Caused by the inherent complexity of the material.
Example:	Learners need more processing to represent a complicated topic such as how lightning storms develop.

Generative processing

Definition:	Deep cognitive processing during learning required to make sense of the presented material (including organizing and integrating).
Cause:	Caused by the learner's motivation to make an effort to learn.
Example:	Learners try harder to relate material to their prior knowledge when the tutor uses conversational style.

Extraneous processing wastes precious cognitive capacity and is caused by poor instructional design (or poor learner strategies). Essential processing is required to represent the material in working memory (such as by selecting and organizing relevant material as presented) and is caused by the complexity of the material (such as the number of interrelated concepts that must be held in working memory at one time). Generative processing is required to make sense of the material in working memory (such as by reorganizing and integrating) and is caused by the learner's motivation to learn. This triarchic theory of instruction is based on the cognitive theory of multimedia learning as described in my book, *Multimedia Learning*, and on Cognitive Load Theory as described in John Sweller's book, *Instructional Design in Technical Areas*.

Meaningful learning requires that the learner engage in appropriate cognitive processing during learning, including selecting relevant material for further processing, organizing the selected material into a coherent mental structure, and integrating the material with prior knowledge from long-term memory. As shown in the following table, extraneous processing does not involve any of the three cognitive processes for meaningful learning; essential processing involves selecting and in some cases some preliminary organizing necessary to represent the material in its presented organization; and generative processing involves reorganizing the new material more extensively and integrating the new structures with each other and with prior knowledge. As you can see, meaningful learning requires that the learner engage in essential and generative processing, whereas rote learning requires only essential processing.

How the Three Kinds of Processing Demands Relate to Learning Outcomes		
Processing Demand	**Cognitive Processes**	**Learning Outcome**
Extraneous processing	Inappropriate processes	No learning
Essential processing	Selecting (and initial organizing)	Rote learning
Generative processing	Organizing and integrating	Meaningful learning

How Instruction Works: Three Instructional Scenarios

Let's consider three possible scenarios for how the three kinds of processing mesh with a learner's cognitive capacity.

What Is Extraneous Overload?

The first scenario involves *extraneous overload,* in which the learner needs to engage in extraneous processing, essential processing, and generative processing but only has sufficient cognitive capacity to support extraneous processing and perhaps a small amount of essential processing. The learner is not able to engage the required amount of essential processing and generative processing, so the learning outcome suffers. To address the problem of extraneous overload, an important instructional goal is to reduce extraneous processing.

Extraneous Overload: Too Much Extraneous Processing		
Required: Extraneous processing	Essential processing	Generative processing
Available: Cognitive Capacity		

What Is Essential Overload?

In the second scenario, called *essential overload,* extraneous processing has been reduced or eliminated, but the demands of essential processing are greater than the learner's cognitive capacity—perhaps because the to-be-learned material is complex and unfamiliar. The learner is not able to engage in the required amount of essential processing and generative processing, so the learning outcome suffers. To address the problem of essential overload, an important instructional goal is to manage essential processing—that is, to reduce its impact on cognitive capacity.

Essential Overload: Too Much Essential Processing		
Required:	Essential processing	Generative processing
Available:	Cognitive Capacity	

What Is Generative Underutilization?

The third scenario is called *generative underutilization*—the learner actually has cognitive capacity available (even after engaging in essential processing) but does not use it fully for generative processing. In this scenario, the learner lacks motivation to process the material more deeply. Thus, an important instructional goal is to foster generative processing.

Generative Underutilization: Not Enough Generative Processing		
Required:	Essential processing	Generative processing
Available:	Cognitive Capacity	

When learners experience extraneous overload, instructional designers should seek ways to reduce extraneous processing so that learners can free up cognitive capacity to be used for essential and generative processing. When learners experience essential overload, instructional designers should seek ways to manage essential processing so that learners free up cognitive capacity to be used for essential and generative processing. When learners experience generative underutilization, instructional designers should seek ways to foster generative processing so that learners use their available cognitive capacity for both essential and generative processing.

Three Top-Level Goals for the Design of Instruction

1. Reduce extraneous processing
2. Manage essential processing
3. Foster generative processing

Twelve Instructional Design Principles for Lesson Learning

In addition to priming appropriate cognitive processes during learning, instructional methods should be sensitive to the learner's cognitive load. The tables in this section list what I consider to be the 12 best-established principles of instructional design for passive learning situations—such as reading a book, attending a lecture, or receiving an online presentation. Each principle is based on research evidence, as documented in one or more of three recent reports: (1) a handbook edited by me describing evidence-based principles for multimedia learning, (2) an Association for Psychological Science task force report on research-based learning principles applied to education, edited by Diane Halpern, Art Graesser, and Milt Hakel, and (3) an Institute of Education Sciences practice guide containing research-based recommendations for improving instruction and studying, written by Harold Pashler and colleagues.

Evidence-Based Instructional Principles for Reducing Extraneous Processing

Sometimes a lesson demands more cognitive processing than the learner's cognitive capacity can accommodate, so an important goal is to help the learner refrain from extraneous processing—cognitive processing that is not related to the instructional objective.

Evidence-Based Instructional Principles for Reducing Extraneous Processing		
Principle	**Description**	**Example**
Coherence [1,2]	People learn better when extraneous material is excluded rather than included.	Cut out interesting but irrelevant text and graphics.
Signaling [1]	People learn better when the organization of a lesson is highlighted.	Use outlines and section headings for a text lesson.
Spatial contiguity [1,2,3]	People learn better when corresponding printed words and pictures are near rather than far from each other on the screen or page.	Embed relevant words within an illustration rather than as a caption.
Temporal contiguity [1,2]	People learn better when corresponding spoken words and pictures are presented simultaneously rather than successively.	Present narration at the same time as animation rather than before or after.
Expectation [2]	People learn better when they are shown in advance the type of test items.	Tell people that after reading this section, they will be asked to give examples of instructional principles.

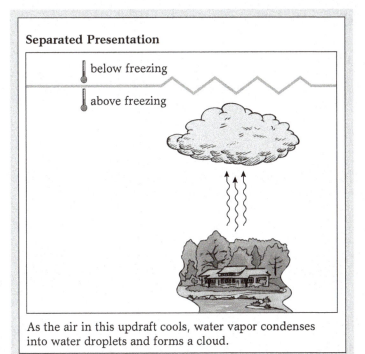

Separated Presentation

below freezing

above freezing

As the air in this updraft cools, water vapor condenses into water droplets and forms a cloud.

Example of the Spatial Contiguity Principle

As an example, let's consider a captioned animation about how lightning storms develop. For example the first slide shows the caption at the bottom of the screen, which I call *separated presentation*.

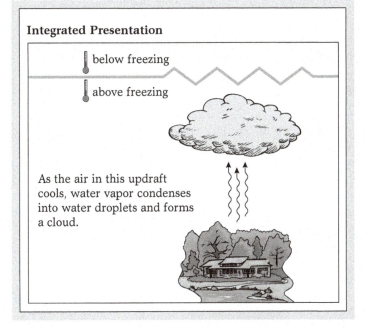

Integrated Presentation

below freezing

above freezing

As the air in this updraft cools, water vapor condenses into water droplets and forms a cloud.

Separated presentation can cause extraneous processing because the learner must scan back and forth between the text and the relevant portion of the graphic. In contrast, we can reduce the amount of extraneous processing by placing the text next to the portion of the graphic that it describes, as exemplified in the second slide. I call this *integrated presentation* because the corresponding words and graphics are near each other on the screen, as called for in the spatial contiguity principle. In this way, we can reduce the amount of extraneous processing.

Evidence-Based Instructional Principles for Managing Essential Processing

Even if we eliminate all extraneous processing, the material may be so complex that the amount of essential processing overloads the learner's cognitive system. In this case instruction should manage essential processing—cognitive processing needed to mentally represent the material. Three evidence-based approaches are to break the lesson into bite-size parts (i.e., segmenting), provide the learner with relevant prior knowledge (i.e., pretraining), and offload some of the visual material from the visual channel to the auditory channel (i.e., modality). In this way, the learner is better able to process the essential material without overloading working memory.

Evidence-Based Instructional Principles for Managing Essential Processing		
Principle	**Description**	**Example**
Segmenting [1,2]	People learn better when a complex lesson is presented in manageable parts.	Break a narrated animation into small segments, each with a *Continue* button.
Pretraining [1]	People learn better from a complex lesson when they receive pretraining in the names and characteristics of the key concepts.	Tell people about the names, locations, and characteristics of the parts before showing them a narrated animation.
Modality [1,3]	People learn better from a multimedia presentation when words are spoken rather than printed.	Accompany an animation with a spoken description rather than onscreen captions.

Example of the Segmenting Principle

Suppose we have a narrated animation on lightning formation that runs as a *continuous presentation* for about two and a half minutes. This continuous presentation might go by so fast that learners are not able to pinpoint the 16 main steps and their cause-and-effect relation to one another. In short, learners may not have the cognitive capacity to support the essential processing needed to build a causal model of how lightning works.

To help manage the learner's essential processing, we can break the lesson into 16 segments, each containing about 10 seconds of animation and a corresponding sentence or two. After each segment, a *Continue* button appears in the bottom right corner of the screen. When the learner clicks on the *Continue* button, the next segment is presented. In this *segmented presentation,* the learner can control the pacing of the presentation.

As you can see the segmented presentation is intended to manage essential processing by allowing the learner to fully digest one step in the causal chain before moving on to the next one.

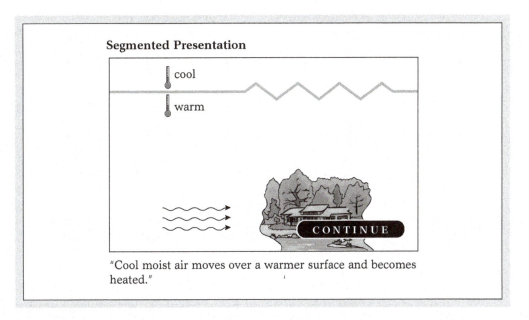

"Cool moist air moves over a warmer surface and becomes heated."

Evidence-Based Instructional Principles for Fostering Generative Processing

Sometimes learners may have cognitive capacity available but are not motivated to exert the extra effort to make sense of the presented material. In this case, instruction should foster generative processing—cognitive processing such as integrating incoming material with existing knowledge.

Evidence-Based Instructional Principles for Fostering Generative Processing		
Principle	**Description**	**Example**
Multimedia [1,2,3]	People learn better from words and pictures than from words alone.	Add relevant graphics to text lesson.
Personalization [1]	People learn better when the instructor uses conversational style rather than formal style.	Use "I" and "you" rather than third-person constructions.
Concretizing [2,3]	People learn better when unfamiliar material is related to familiar knowledge.	Provide concrete examples or analogies; encourage relevant motor activity.
Anchoring [2,3]	People learn better when material is presented in the context of a familiar situation.	Let children learn about arithmetic by having to make change in a play store.

It is important to note that each principle has boundary conditions concerning applicability. For example, most of these principles apply to inexperienced learners rather than experienced learners. Slava Kalyuga coined the term *expertise reversal effect* to refer to the finding that some instructional design principles effective for beginners are ineffective or even detrimental for experts. Overall, the principles should be used in ways that are consistent with a cognitive theory of how people learn.

Example of Multimedia Principle

For example, we can explain how a bicycle tire pump works by asking the learner to click on a speaker icon in order to hear the narration: "When the handle is pulled up, the piston moves up, the inlet valve opens, the outlet valve closes, and air enters the lower part of the cylinder." The words are somewhat abstract and the learner may not be motivated to engage in generative processing such as connecting the verbal explanation with other knowledge. To help foster generative processing, we can add pictures—such as a short animation—to the narration, creating a narrated animation. Below are some selected frames from the animation along with the words that were spoken. In my book *Multimedia Learning*, I have summarized numerous studies demonstrating that people learn more deeply from words and pictures than from words alone, thereby supporting the *multimedia principle.*

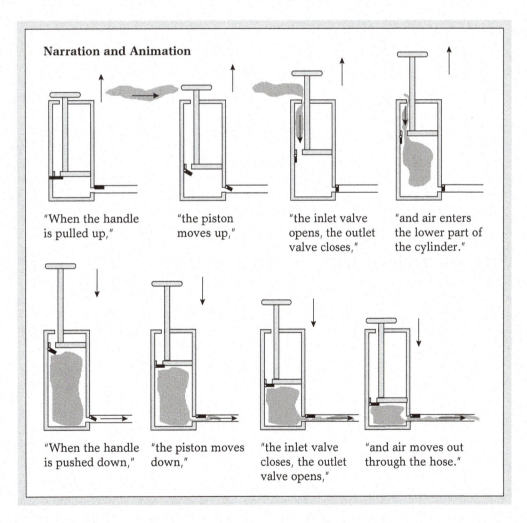

Narration and Animation

"When the handle is pulled up,"

"the piston moves up,"

"the inlet valve opens, the outlet valve closes,"

"and air enters the lower part of the cylinder."

"When the handle is pushed down,"

"the piston moves down,"

"the inlet valve closes, the outlet valve opens,"

"and air moves out through the hose."

Eight Instructional Design Principles for Effective Studying

In the previous section (pp. 66–71), we explored 12 evidence-based principles for how to design a lesson that presents information to a learner—such as in the form of a book, lecture, or online presentation. In this section, let's consider ways to encourage studying behaviors that lead to successful learning. In the following tables, I summarize what I consider to be the eight best-supported principles for studying (along with the sources indicated in brackets).

Evidence-Based Principles for Studying by Practicing

The first set of four principles concerns studying by practicing—that is, studying by performing the to-be-learned task. When you practice performing a task, the best ways to learn are to space out the practice (i.e., spacing), to receive prompt explanations of correct performance after you perform (i.e., feedback), to have correct performance on similar tasks modeled for you before you perform (i.e., worked examples), and to receive appropriate guidance as you perform (i.e., guided discovery).

Evidence-Based Principles for Practicing		
Principle	**Description**	**Example**
Spacing [2,3]	People learn better when they spread out practice over several shorter sessions rather than massing practice in one longer session.	The learner practices addition problems for 10 minutes a day for 5 days rather than for 50 minutes in 1 day.
Feedback [2]	People learn better from practice when they receive explanative feedback on their performance.	After solving a word problem, the learner receives a step-by-step explanation of how to solve it.
Worked example [1,3]	People learn better when worked examples are presented before to-be-solved problems.	The learner sees a step-by-step solution for $3x - 5 = 4$ (with explanations for each step), and then solves $2a - 2 = 6$.
Guided discovery [1,2]	When performing a task, people learn better with guidance such as modeling, coaching, and scaffolding rather than by pure discovery.	As the learner attempts to solve a word problem, the teacher provides hints, circles the important numbers, and tells how she thinks about planning a solution.

Example of the Worked Example Principle

Suppose students have read a textbook lesson on how to solve algebra equations and we now want to give them some practice. A seemingly straightforward approach would be to ask students to solve a few problems such as shown below on the left. In contrast, we could provide a worked example and then pair it with a problem to solve as shown below on the right.

Learning By Doing
Solve each equation for a:

$a + b = c$

$a + h = u$

$a - b = c$

$a - v = f$

$a + b - g = c$

$a + e - v = s$

$a - b + g = c$

$a - r + y = k$

Learning By Example
Use each worked example to help you solve the next equation for a:

$$\boxed{\begin{array}{l} a + b = c \\ \quad a = c - b \end{array}}$$

$a + h = u$

$$\boxed{\begin{array}{l} a - b = c \\ \quad a = c + b \end{array}}$$

$a - v = f$

$$\boxed{\begin{array}{l} a + b - g = c \\ \quad a + b = c + g \\ \qquad a = c + g - b \end{array}}$$

$a + e - v = s$

$$\boxed{\begin{array}{l} a - b + g = c \\ \quad a + g = c + b \\ \qquad a = c + b - g \end{array}}$$

$a - r + y = k$

Research by Graham Cooper and John Sweller shows that learning by example is more effective than learning by doing in promoting transfer test performance, thus providing evidence for the worked example principle. Although the learner is behaviorally active in learning by doing, worked examples help guide the learner's cognitive processing.

Evidence-Based Principles for Studying by Generating

The second set of four principles concerns studying by generating—engaging in learning-inducing activities during learning from a presentation. When you have an otherwise passive lesson, you can test yourself by trying to recall the material (i.e., testing), you can explain the material to yourself (i.e., self-explanation), you can generate and answer questions based on the material (i.e., questioning), and you can summarize or outline or otherwise produce elaborations on the material (i.e., elaboration).

Evidence-Based Principles for Generating		
Principle	**Description**	**Example**
Testing [2,3]	People learn better from taking practice tests than from restudying.	After reading a textbook lesson on how digestion works, the learner tries to write down all the steps in the process rather than restudying the lesson.
Self-explanation [1,2,3]	People learn better when they explain lesson elements to themselves during learning.	As they read a textbook lesson on how the heart works, learners comment on ideas that conflict with their conception and try to explain the system in their own words.
Questioning [2,3]	People learn better when they must ask and answer deep questions during learning.	After viewing each section of a narrated animation on geology, the learner generates and answers deep questions of the form "What caused Y?", "How does X compare to Y?" or "What if?"
Elaboration [2]	People learn better when they outline, summarize, or elaborate on the presented material.	The learner takes summary notes while listening to a lecture.

As you can see, these principles tend to encourage deeper cognitive processing, which I call *generative processing*.

Example of the Self-Explanation Principle

Suppose you are viewing a computer screen that contains a lesson on the human visual system. The lesson consists of text in one window and illustrations in another, but you are able to view only one window at a time. If you are like most learners, you may read through the text and then look over the illustrations. This approach to studying does not do much to encourage you to engage in generative processing, so the result may be that you memorize the material as presented.

In contrast, consider a studying context in which you are asked to think aloud as you view the material, in an attempt to explain the material to yourself. For example, let's look in on a learner who has just read the sentence "The shape of the cornea is responsible for about 70% of the eye's focusing power." Here's what the learner says and does next:

Self-Explanation Transcript

"So I am wondering what's the other 30%."

Toggle to illustration of parts of the eye.

"Okay, so now I understand. I always thought that there's just the lens and that the cornea and the lens were the same thing. But now I realize that it's the lens that actually does the rest of the work. I though it was all the cornea or all the lens cause I thought it was the same thing. Okay, now I am actually learning something."

This transcript comes from research by Marguerite Roy and Michelene Chi reported in *The Cambridge Handbook of Multimedia Learning* (pp. 277–278). Consistent with the self-explanation principle, learner-generated explanations can help learners monitor and repair their knowledge. In short, self-explanation is a form of studying by generating in which appropriate learner activity during a lesson can lead to deeper learning.

How to Guide Cognitive Processes during Learning

Meaningful learning occurs when the learner engages in three important cognitive processes during learning:

1. *Selecting*: Paying attention to relevant information in the lesson
2. *Organizing*: Mentally arranging the selected information into a coherent mental representation
3. *Integrating*: Mentally connecting the mental representation with relevant prior knowledge retrieved from long-term memory

Let's consider some instructional techniques that are intended to prime each of these cognitive processes during learning.

Instructional Techniques for Selecting

First, the following table lists examples of techniques intended to prime the process of selecting. Each technique has been shown to be effective in increasing retention of the emphasized material.

Instructional Techniques Intended to Guide the Process of Selecting		
Technique	**Description**	**Explanation**
Objectives	Statements of what the learner should learn from the lesson.	Learner focuses on parts of the lesson that help achieve the objective.
Pre-questions	Questions inserted before each section of a lesson for the learner to answer.	Learner focuses on parts of the lesson that help answer the question.
Post-questions	Questions inserted after each section of a lesson for the learner to answer.	Learner develops an expectation for a certain type of question, so focuses on information in the lesson for that type of question.
Highlighting	Emphasis on certain words in a lesson by use of different font size, style, color, bolding, italics, underlining, flashing, etc.	Learner focuses on words that look different from the others.

As an example, consider a textbook or multimedia lesson on how an electric motor works. The lesson has five sections, each focusing on the role of a main component in the motor—the battery, the wires, the commutator, the wire loop, or the magnets. The following table shows how we can implement each of the exemplary techniques for guiding the learner's attention during learning about electric motors.

Examples of Instructional Techniques for Selecting

Technique	Example in a Lesson on How an Electric Motor Works
Objectives	Before the lesson: "In this lesson you will learn to locate the five main parts in an electric motor."
Pre-questions	Before the lesson: "Suppose you turn on an electric motor but it does not work. What could have gone wrong?"
Post-questions	After the first section: "What is the function of the battery?"
	After the second section: "What is the function of the wires?"
	After the third section: "What is the function of the commutator?"
	After the fourth section: "What is the function of the wire loop?"
	After the fifth section: "What is the function of the magnets?"
Highlighting	Within the lesson: "When the motor is switched on, electrons flow out of the battery through the **negative terminal** and electrons flow into the battery through the **positive terminal.**"

Although it is important to guide the learner's attention during learning, this is only the first step in fostering meaningful learning. If we stopped here, the learner would be left with a collection of seemingly isolated fragments to memorize. The next two cognitive processes—organizing and integrating—are crucial for helping the learner construct a meaningful learning outcome. Furthermore, instructional techniques that foster organizing and integrating may also guide the learner's attention.

Instructional Techniques for Organizing

Second, the following table lists examples of techniques intended to prime the process of organizing. Each technique is a component in *signaling*, which has been shown to be effective in increasing retention of the emphasized material and in increasing transfer test performance.

Instructional Techniques Intended to Guide the Process of Organizing		
Technique	**Description**	**Explanation**
Outline	A sentence in the introduction that lists the sections of the lesson or a list of sections at the beginning of the lesson; the items in the list should be concise and in parallel structure.	Outlines give the learner a road map for where the lesson is going and a set of labels for segmenting the lesson into parts.
Headings	Highlighted words at the start of each section that are keyed to the outline.	Headings help the learner organize the material within a coherent structure.
Pointer words	Words such as "first . . . second . . . third" or "in contrast" or "as a result."	Pointer words help the learner identify the local structure of events or elements in the lesson.
Graphic organizer	A matrix or hierarchy or network that shows the key concepts in a spatial layout.	Graphic organizers pinpoint the key elements and their relations for the learner.

As you can see, each technique is intended to help the learner build an organized structure for the material in the lesson. For example, consider our electric motor lesson. The table shows how we can implement each of the exemplary techniques for guiding the learner's process of organizing during learning with this lesson.

Examples of Instructional Techniques for Organizing

	Example in the Electric Motor Lesson
Outline	Before the lesson: "In this lesson you will learn about the workings of each of the five parts of an electric motor: battery, wires, commutator, wire loop, and magnets."
Headings	Before first section: **How the Battery Works**
	Before second section: **How the Wires Work**
	Before third section: **How the Commutator Works**
	Before fourth section: **How the Wire Loop Works**
	Before fifth section: **How the Magnets Works**
Pointer words	Within the lesson: "First, when the motor is in the start position . . .
	Second, when the motor has rotated a quarter turn . . .
	Third, when the motor has rotated a half turn . . .
	Fourth, when the motor has rotated three quarters of a turn . . .
	Fifth, when the motor has rotated a full turn . . ."

Graphic organizer	**Steps in the Working of the Battery**	
	Step	**What Happens**
	Start position	Electrons flow from negative terminal; electrons flow to positive terminal.
	Quarter turn	Electrons stop flowing.
	Half turn	Electrons flow from negative terminal; electrons flow to positive terminal.
	Three-quarters turn	Electrons stop flowing.
	Full turn	Same as start position.

Instructional Techniques for Integrating

Third, the following table lists two exemplary techniques intended to prime the process of integrating—helping learners connect what is presented with they already know. Each is based on creating a metaphor in which learners understand a new (or abstract) system in terms of a familiar (or concrete) system that they already know about. Both techniques have been shown to be effective in improving learner understanding as indicated by increased learner retention and transfer test performance.

Instructional Techniques Intended to Guide the Process of Integrating		
Technique	**Description**	**Explanation**
Concrete advance organizer	Familiar material presented before a lesson intended to promote deep learning.	Learner activates relevant prior knowledge and uses it to assimilate new material.
Concrete model	Familiar material presented during a lesson intended to promote deep learning.	Learner activates relevant prior knowledge and uses it to assimilate new material.

For example, a lesson on how electrical circuits work may be somewhat abstract and unfamiliar. To help the learner make sense out of the lesson, a concrete advance organizer could explicitly show how an electrical circuit is like water flowing in pipes, as shown in the following illustration.

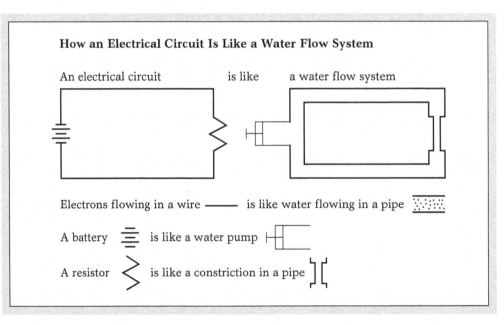

As another example, consider a lesson in which students learn how to compute answers to two-digit subtraction problems. The subtraction procedure can be abstract and unfamiliar material for children; so to provide a concrete context we can show how the subtraction procedure works using a concrete and familiar context such as bundles of sticks.

Example of Using a Concrete Model to Teach an Abstract Procedure

Abstract Instruction

Concrete Instruction

"Fifty-three minus twenty-nine"

$$\begin{array}{r} 53 \\ -29 \end{array}$$

"You have five bundles of ten sticks each, and three individual sticks. You need to take away twenty-nine sticks."

"Start in the units column. You can't take nine from three so you borrow one from the five, change it to four. Add ten to the three, make it thirteen. Subtract nine from thirteen, put 4 here."

$$\begin{array}{r} \overset{4}{\cancel{5}}\overset{13}{3} \\ -29 \\ \hline 4 \end{array}$$

"You can't take nine sticks away from three sticks, so you untie one of the bundles of ten sticks. This leaves you with four bundles of ten sticks and thirteen individual sticks.

"Now we can take away nine sticks from the thirteen individual sticks, leaving four sticks.

"Shift to the tens column. Subtract two from four, put 2 here. The answer is twenty-four."

$$\begin{array}{r} \overset{4}{\cancel{5}}\overset{13}{3} \\ -29 \\ \hline 24 \end{array}$$

"Next, we need to take away twenty sticks so we take away two bundles of ten sticks, leaving two bundles of ten sticks. The answer is twenty-four."

In this section, you have seen some selected examples of techniques for promoting the cognitive processes of selecting, organizing, and integrating. I selected them because each clearly targeted one of the processes. In the previous two sections (pp. 66–75) you found other instructional methods that are effective because they also prime these cognitive processes during learning.

Three Popular but Questionable Principles

You might have expected to see three other popular principles on the list: collaboration, discovery, and learning styles. I have reserved them for the end because they need special treatment.

Questions about Collaborative Learning

Collaborative learning occurs when a group is a given a challenging problem, task, or project to carry out on their own. For example, a group may engage in discussion as they come up with a group product such as working together in a group of four to create a class presentation on the cognitive effects of video games. A recent review by Robert Slavin, Eric Hurley, and Anne Chamberlain in the *Handbook of Psychology* pinpoints forms of collaboration that are and are not supported by classroom research. As you can see, it is not always helpful to study in groups.

What Works with Collaboration?

Effective?	Collaboration Context
Yes	*Cooperative learning:* group reward based on individual members' performance, such as each group member taking a test and the sum of the scores (or improvements in score) counting as the group grade given to all group members.
Yes	*Reciprocal teaching:* group members take turns teaching specific cognitive skills with guidance from the teacher, so each group member gets a chance to see what it feels like to be the teacher.
Questionable	*Group project:* group reward based on a single group product or no group reward, such as a single grade given to all group members for a group presentation in class.
Questionable	*Group discovery:* group works together to solve problems without guidance from the teacher, such as a group of students working unassisted on math homework problems.

Questions about Discovery Learning

Discovery learning occurs when a learner is given a challenging problem, task, or project to carry out on his or her own. The learner may seek out instruction as he or she comes up with a product. For example, developing an entry for a science fair is an example of discovery learning. In a recent review of research entitled "Should There Be a Three-Strikes Rule against Pure Discovery Learning?" I concluded "there is sufficient research evidence to make any reasonable person skeptical about the benefits of discovery learning" (p. 14). Indeed, research has repeatedly shown that inexperienced learners need guidance as they practice a new task, including coaching, scaffolding, modeling, questioning, and feedback. For each of these guidance techniques, the following table provides a description and example based on the subtraction problem 64 – 25 = ___.

Some Types of Guidance in Guided Discovery

Type	Description	Example
Coaching	Providing relevant information, advice, and hints for how to carry out a task	"Let's rewrite the problem so 64 is on top and 25 is on bottom. Remember the right column is units and the left column is tens."
Scaffolding	Providing an easier version of the task or breaking the problem into parts	"OK, the first few steps are worked out for you, so what is the next step?"
Modeling	Showing how to do the task along with explanations	"Here's how I solve the problem . . ."
Questioning	Asking the learner to explain or justify what they are doing	"Why did you write a 1 next to the 4?"
Feedback	Providing an explanation of correct performance, in response to the learner's performance	"Let's start with the units column."

Questions about Learning Style

Some people are verbal learners and they should be taught with words; some people are visual learners and they should be taught with pictures; some people are auditory learners and they should be taught with sounds. These kinds of statements reflect the *learning style principle*—the idea that people should receive instructional methods that correspond to their learning styles. Learning style refers to the way that a learner tends to process information. Although the learning style principle has popular appeal and is part of the folklore of teacher education, there is not much convincing evidence to support its widespread implementation in schools.

For example, suppose we gave a questionnaire to students intended to assess whether they were visualizers or verbalizers. As an example, the following one-item survey was developed by Laura Massa and me to determine a learner's verbalizer–visualizer learning style:

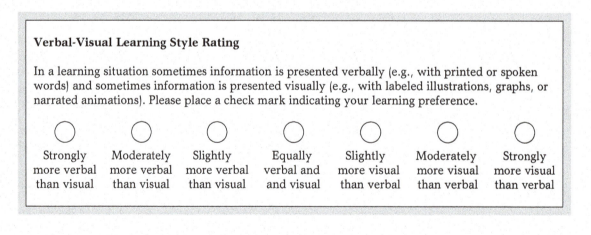

Verbal-Visual Learning Style Rating

In a learning situation sometimes information is presented verbally (e.g., with printed or spoken words) and sometimes information is presented visually (e.g., with labeled illustrations, graphs, or narrated animations). Please place a check mark indicating your learning preference.

○ Strongly more verbal than visual ○ Moderately more verbal than visual ○ Slightly more verbal than visual ○ Equally verbal and and visual ○ Slightly more visual than verbal ○ Moderately more visual than verbal ○ Strongly more visual than verbal

If the learning style principle were correct, you would expect visualizers to perform better on a test after studying a visually based lesson whereas verbalizers should perform better on a test after studying a verbally based lesson—as shown in the graph on the left. In contrast, when Laura Massa and I conducted just such a study, we found results that were more like the graph on the right side of the figure—both verbalizers and visualizers did about the same with a verbally based lesson and both did about the same with a visually based lesson. Like many other studies on the visualizer–verbalizer style dimension, there was no evidence to support the learning style principle. Until there is a supportive evidence base, it is best to be skeptical of recommendations to individualize instruction based on learning style.

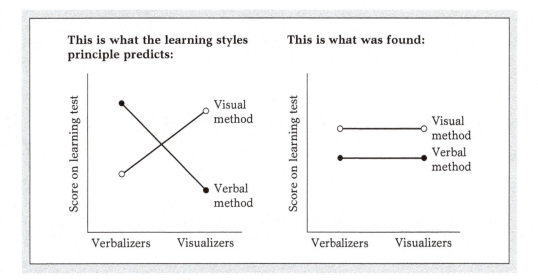

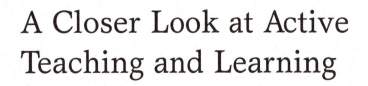

A Closer Look at Active Teaching and Learning

How Active Teaching Methods Can Go Wrong

Although active teaching methods such as discovery and collaboration are in common use, they may be used in ways that can harm learning. As shown in the following table, both activities are intended to foster generative processing—which is a laudable goal. For example, they encourage the learner to search relevant existing knowledge to help make sense of the to-be-learned material. However, unstructured exploration or discussion by novices can be somewhat inefficient, leading to an increase in extraneous processing—cognitive processing that is not related to the instructional goal. At the same time, learners may fail to come into contact with the to-be-learned material and hence are less able to engage in essential processing—building a mental representation of the essential material. When the benefits of discovery or collaboration (in terms of increased generative processing) are offset by their costs (in terms of increased extraneous processing and decreased essential processing), the use of these instructional methods becomes questionable.

How Discovery and Collaboration Can Go Wrong

Activity	Cognitive Processing		
	Extraneous	*Essential*	*Generative*
Discovery	Increases	Decreases	Increases
Collaboration	Increases	Decreases	Increases

The goal for using discovery and collaboration is a worthwhile one—to encourage meaningful learning. However, research shows that this goal is often unmet when instructors use pure discovery and ineffective forms of collaboration. The challenge for instructional designers is to use methods that prime generative processing but provide enough guidance to make sure learners engage in appropriate amounts of essential processing and do not engage in excessive amounts of extraneous processing.

Two Kinds of Active Learning

A rationale for using discovery or collaborative methods is that they foster active learning—the learner is actively doing and discussing. However, not all kinds of active learning promote learning. The following illustration shows two kinds of active learning—behavioral activity (such as hands-on activity or discussion) and cognitive activity (which involves the cognitive processes of selecting, organizing, and integrating). As you can see, it is the level of cognitive activity that causes learning whereas high behavioral activity does not necessarily promote learning better than low behavioral activity. As shown in the upper-right quadrant, it is possible to have meaningful learning with low levels of behavioral activity (perhaps, exemplified by your reading of this page). In contrast, as shown in the lower-left quadrant, it is possible to not have meaningful learning with high levels of behavioral activity (such as rotely following a procedure in a hands-on science lab demonstration).

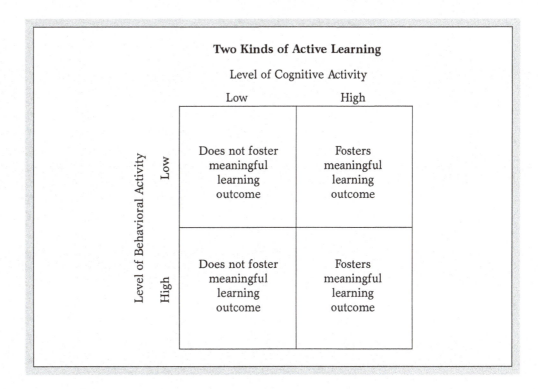

References and Suggested Readings

Pages 54–55

Shavelson, R. J., & Towne, L. (Eds.). (2002). *Scientific research in education.* Washington, DC: National Academy Press.

A consensus document summarizing six principles for conducting scientific research in education.

Pages 56–61

Anderson, L. W., Krathwohl, D. R., Airasian, P. W., Cruikshank, K. A., Mayer, R. E., Pintrich, P. R., Raths, J., & Wittrock, M. C. (2001). *A taxonomy for learning, teaching, and assessing: A revision of Bloom's taxonomy of educational objectives.* New York: Longman.

A framework for creating instructional objectives based on advances in the science of learning, written by a team of experts in learning, instruction, and assessment.

Pellegrino, J. W., Chudowsky, N., & Glaser, R. (Eds.). (2001). *Knowing what students know: The science and design of educational assessment.* Washington, DC: National Academy Press.

A careful analysis of how to assess learning outcomes commissioned by the National Research Council and written by leading assessment researchers.

Pages 62–65

Mayer, R. E. (2009). *Multimedia learning* (2nd ed.). New York: Cambridge University Press.

Reviews a program of research on effective instructional methods based on the science of learning.

Sweller, J. (1999). *Instructional design in technical areas.* Camberwell, Australia: ACER Press.

Reviews a program of research based on cognitive load theory.

Pages 66–75

Clark, R. C., & Mayer, R. E. (2008). *e-Learning and the science of instruction.* San Francisco: Pfeiffer.

Reviews research on effective instructional methods in computer-based environments.

Cooper, G., & Sweller, J. (1987). The effects of schema acquisition and rule automation on mathematical problem-solving transfer. *Journal of Educational Psychology, 79,* 347–362.

A research study on the instructional effects of worked-out examples.

Halpern, D. F., Graesser, A., & Hakel, M. (2007). *25 learning principles to guide pedagogy and the design of learning environments.* Washington, DC: American Psychological Society Taskforce on Life Long Learning at Work and at Home. [http://psyc.memphis.edu/learning]

Reviews 25 research-based principles for instructional design. Listed as [2] in the text.

Kalyuga, S. (2005). Prior knowledge principle in multimedia learning. In R. E. Mayer (Ed.), *The Cambridge handbook of multimedia learning* (pp. 325–338). New York: Cambridge University Press.

A summary of research on the expertise reversal effect.

Mayer, R. E. (Ed.). (2005). *The Cambridge handbook of multimedia learning,* New York: Cambridge University Press.

Contains 35 chapters reviewing research on principles of instructional design of multimedia instruction. Listed as [1] in the text.

Mayer, R. E. (2009). *Multimedia learning* (2nd ed.). New York: Cambridge University Press.

Reviews a program of research on effective instructional methods based on the science of learning.

O'Neil, H. F. (Ed.). (2005). *What works in distance learning: Guidelines*. Greenwich, CT: Information Age Publishing.

Summarizes research-based principles for instructional design of online lessons.

Pashler, H., Bain, P., Bottage, B., Graesser, A., Koedinger, K., McDaniel, M., & Metcalfe, J. (2007). *Organizing instruction and study to improve student learning* (NCER 2007–2004). Washington, DC: National Center for Educational Research, Institute of Educational Sciences, U.S. Department of Education. [http://ncer.ed.gov]

Reviews research-based principles for instructional design. Listed as [3] in the text.

Roy, M., & Chi, M. T. H. (2005). The self-explanation principle in multimedia learning. In R. E. Mayer (Ed.), *The Cambridge handbook of multimedia learning* (pp. 271–286). New York: Cambridge University Press.

A review of research on the effectiveness of self-explanation as an instructional method.

Pages 76–81

Mayer, R. E. (2008). *Learning and instruction* (2nd ed.). Upper Saddle River, NJ: Pearson/Merrill Prentice Hall.

An up-to-date summary of research on instructional methods that foster meaningful learning.

Pages 82–85

Mayer, R. E. (2004). Should there be a three-strikes rule against pure discovery learning? *American Psychologist, 59*, 14–19.

A review of research on discovery learning.

Mayer, R. E., & Massa, L. J. (2003). Three facets of visual and verbal learners: Cognitive ability, cognitive style, and learning preference. *Journal of Educational Psychology, 95*, 833–846.

The source of the verbal-visual learning style rating.

Slavin, R. E., Hurley, E. A., & Chamberlain, A. (2003). Cooperative learning and achievement: Theory and research. In W. M. Reynolds & G. E. Miller (Eds.), *Handbook of psychology* (vol. 7; pp. 177–198). New York: Wiley.

A review of research on learning in groups.

Section 3

How Assessment Works

A central task in applying the science of learning involves assessment of learning outcomes—that is, what James Pellegrino and colleagues call "knowing what students know." Assessment is sometimes viewed as a separate activity added on to the end of an educational program. In contrast, the approach I take in this book assumes that assessment is inextricably connected with learning and instruction. Assessment is linked to learning because it helps to clearly describe what is learned, and assessment is linked to instruction because it helps guide instruction.

If we wish to take a scientific approach to learning, we need empirical evidence to test our theories of learning. If we wish to take a scientific approach to instruction, we need empirical evidence to determine which instructional method is most effective. The science of assessment enables us to generate this evidence.

The science of assessment is concerned with determining what a learner knows. In this section, I introduce you to the concepts and issues in the assessment of learning outcomes.

Bite-Size Chunks of the Science of Assessment

What Is Assessment?

What Is the Science of Assessment?

Three Functions of Assessments

How to Construct a Useful Assessment Instrument

What Is Research on Instructional Effects?

    What Works? Using Randomized Controlled Experiments

    When Does It Work? Using Factorial Experiments

    How Does It Work? Using Observational Analysis

A Closer Look at Experiments

    Using Effect Size to Assess Instructional Effects

    Six Reasons for No Difference between the Treatment and Control Groups

How to Assess Learning Outcomes

    Two Ways to Measure Learning Outcomes

    Three Kinds of Learning Outcomes

A Closer Look at Meaningful versus Rote Learning: Wertheimer's Parallelogram Lesson

A Closer Look at Assessment of Learning Outcomes: How Much or What Kind?

Broadening the Domain of Assessment

A Closer Look at Broadening the Domain of Assessment: Attribute Treatment Interactions

Attribute Treatment Interactions Involving Prior Knowledge

What Can Go Wrong with Assessments?

What Is Assessment?

Assessment involves determining what a learner has learned, the way the learner learned the material, or the learner's characteristics related to learning. When we conduct an assessment, we seek to describe someone's learning outcome (i.e., knowledge), learning processes (i.e., cognitive processes for constructing knowledge), or learning characteristics (i.e., capabilities related to constructing knowledge). These three targets of assessment are summarized in the following table. The most common target of assessment is the learner's knowledge, that is, what the learner knows, as indicated in the first row. In short, assessment of learning outcomes is the main focus of this section.

Three Targets of Assessment		
What Is Assessed?	**Description**	**Example**
Learning outcome	What does someone know after instruction?	Write down the definition of *assessment*.
Learning process	How does someone learn during instruction?	Rate your mental effort during the lesson from 1 (very low) to 7 (very high).
Learning characteristics	What is someone like before instruction?	Rate your level of interest in learning about assessment from 1 (very low) to 7 (very high).

Assessment is generally indirect. We observe the learner's performance, such as the answer to a test question. From the learner's performance, we infer the learner's knowledge, processes, or characteristics.

Relation between What the Learner Knows and What the Learner Does

What the learner knows: What the learner does:

| Knowledge | $\longrightarrow$ | Performance |

Assessment: Knowledge enables performance

What Is the Science of Assessment?

In the introduction to this book, we defined the science of assessment, but in this section let's elaborate on that definition.

What is the science of assessment?

Definition: The science of assessment is the scientific study of how to determine what people know.

Goal: Valid and reliable instruments for assessing learning outcomes, learning processes, and learning capabilities.

Criterion: Instruments are valid and reliable.

The science of assessment is the scientific study of how to determine what people know. In a recent report of the National Research Council, entitled *Knowing What Students Know,* James Pellegrino, Naomi Chudowsky, and Robert Glaser made this point as follows:

Educational assessment seeks to determine how well students are learning. (p. 1)

In short, the science of assessment is concerned with designing ways of "knowing what students know."

The primary goal of the science of assessment is to develop instruments (or methods) for determining what a learner has learned—that is, changes in what the learner knows after learning. In addition, in some cases the goal of the science of assessment is to develop instruments (or methods) for determining the cognitive processes that the learner engaged in during learning or to determine the characteristics of the learner before learning.

The main criteria are that the assessment instruments are valid—that is, they are used for an appropriate purpose—and reliable—that is, they give the same measurements when they are administered in the same circumstances.

As you can see, having useful assessment instruments is indispensable in applying the science of learning to education. If we want to develop evidence-based theories of learning and evidence-based principles of instruction, we must be able to assess what people have learned. In short, educational assessments put the "evidence" into "evidence-based practice." A fundamental challenge in educational research involves the development of useful assessment instruments—tests that really tell us what students know.

Three Functions of Assessment

Assessment is intrinsically related to instruction. In particular, assessment can be used for three instructional functions—*before instruction,* to describe a learner's characteristics; *during instruction,* to describe how a learner is responding to instruction; and *after instruction,* to describe what has been learned. These three functions are summarized in the following table. By far the most common function of assessment is to assess the learner's knowledge after instruction, as indicated in the third row.

Three Functions of Assessment		
When	**Function**	**Example**
Before instruction	To determine the characteristics of the learner in order to plan appropriate instruction	What do you already know?
During instruction	To determine what the learner is learning in order to adjust ongoing instruction	What are you learning from the lesson?
After instruction	To provide accountability by documenting student learning; to provide input for program revision	What did you learn from the instructional unit or course?

As you can see in the first row on assessment before learning (or *pre-assessment*), it is useful to know something about the learner, such as the learner's prior knowledge, interest, and learning ability. For example, at the start of the year in a primary grade mathematics class, we can give learners a pretest to assess their knowledge of basic arithmetic. When you need to make instructional decisions, the single most important individual differences dimension is prior knowledge.

As you can see in the second row, assessment during instruction—also called *formative assessment*—involves determining what someone has learned over a short term, such as a single lesson in a multi-lesson program or a 20-minute segment of an 8-hour workshop. For example, at some point in a lesson, an instructor could give students an informal quiz by writing a problem on the board and asking them to write down and hand in their solutions. Examining the quiz results can help the instructor determine whether the pace and method of instruction are working and pinpoint content areas that need more work.

As you can see in the third row, assessment after instruction—also called *summative assessment*—involves determining what someone has learned over a long term, such as an entire course or program. For example, after a course in algebra, students take a final exam covering the material for the entire course. The exam score provides accountability by documenting the degree to which the course was effective in helping students learn algebra. Assessments after instruction can also suggest areas that might need improvement the next time the course is taught, and thus serve a formative role.

How to Construct a Useful Assessment Instrument

The appropriate use of an assessment instrument (which for simplicity I will call a *test*) has four characteristics:

1. *Valid*. The test score is interpreted and used for an appropriate purpose.
2. *Reliable*. The test consistently yields the same score every time under the same circumstances.
3. *Objective*. The test score is the same for every scorer.
4. *Referenced*. The test score is in a form that it is easily interpreted.

These four characteristics are summarized in the following table.

Four Characteristics of a Useful Test Score		
Characteristic	**Definition**	**Implementation**
Valid	Test score is interpreted and used for an appropriate purpose.	Degree to which test content matches intended content (content-related evidence); correlation between test and future performance on a criterion task (criterion-related evidence)
Reliable	Test gives the same score every time.	Correlation between test and retest (test-retest reliability); correlation between two halves of the test (split-half reliability)
Objective	Test is scored the same way by all scorers.	Correlation between scores of two raters (inter-rater reliability)
Referenced	Test score is interpretable.	Number of standard deviations above or below the mean (standard score); percentage of scores that are below the raw score (percentile rank); whether a criterion is met

Validity depends on the degree to which a test score is interpreted and used for an appropriate purpose. As noted in the *Standards for Educational and Psychological Testing* published in 1999, validity is not a property of a test per se but rather "refers to the degree to which evidence and theory support the interpretations of the test scores entailed by the proposed users of tests" (p. 9). Two sources of evidence concerning validity are content-related evidence and criterion-related evidence. *Content-related evidence* refers to the degree to which the test items cover relevant material (formally called *face validity* or *content validity*). For example, suppose that a test intended to measure addition and subtraction of fractions contained items about geometry—then your use of the test would lack evidence to support its valid use. *Criterion-related evidence* refers to the degree to which a test score is related to future performance on a criterion measure (formally called *predictive validity*). For example, the score on a college admissions test should correlate strongly with college grades. Let's get the admission test scores for 100 students and then get their grade point average for their first two years at college. If there is no strong positive correlation, criterion-related evidence of validity is lacking.

Reliability refers to the consistency of the test score. A reliable test gives the same score under the same circumstances. Two ways of determining a test's reliability are *test-retest reliability* and *split-half reliability*. In test-retest reliability, you ask people to take the test and then at another time you ask them to take it again under identical circumstances. The test is reliable to the degree that the two scores correlate with one another. Suppose 20 students take a spelling test twice on the same 10 words and under the same circumstances, and for many students the second score is much higher or much lower than the first score. In this case, the test is not reliable. In split-half reliability, you compare the score based on half the items with the score based on the other half of the items. In a math test with 20 items, for example, you get the average score for 10 randomly selected items and the average score for the other 10 items for each of 25 students. The test is reliable to the degree that the scores on the two halves correlate. Tests with more items allow for greater reliability, and split-half reliability only works if all the test items tap the same dimension.

Objectivity is another form of reliability, in which the test is scored the same way regardless of the scorer. One way to determine the objectivity of a test is to have two different scorers generate scores for a collection of test takers. For example, for each of 20 test takers you have the scores of both scorers. The test is objective to the degree that the scores of two scorers correlate with one another, a correlation that is called *inter-rater reliability*. When you think of an objective test, you may think of a multiple-choice test. This is a correct assumption because scoring an objective test does not require any judgment on the part of the scorer. However, open-ended questions (such as essay questions) can also be high in objectivity as long as the scoring key (or scoring rubric) is very clear.

Referencing allows you to know what a raw score means. A *norm-referenced* (or standardized) *test* gives you a score that allows you to determine where you stand relative to other test takers. Two common approaches to standardization are *standard scores* and *percentile ranks*. In standard scores, you subtract the mean score from your score and divide by the standard deviation. This converts a raw score into a standard score—a measure of how many standard deviations above or below the mean your score is. A standard score of + 0.8 means that your score is 0.8 standard deviations above the mean. In percentile rank, we convert your raw score into a percentile rank by counting how people scored below you and above you. A percentile rank of 80 means than you scored above 80% of the test takers. As you can see, standard scores allow you to interpret what a raw score means. If you want to be able to interpret a score with respect to other test takers, then standardization is needed. A *criterion-referenced test* tells you whether or not a specific learning objective has been met, such as whether or not the learner can accomplish a specified task. In criterion referencing you set a cut score for performance on a certain set of test items that is supposed to have valid evidence rather than being arbitrarily selected.

What Is Research on Instructional Effects?

In assessing instructional effectiveness, there are three basic types of questions you can ask, each best answered by a different type of research method.

1. *What works?* First, we may just want to know if a particular instructional method is effective. For example, to test the effectiveness of smiling and gesturing during lectures, we can compare the mean test scores of a group that learns from a lecture in which the lecturer smiles and gestures and an equivalent group that learns from an identical lecture from the same lecturer but without smiling and gesturing.
2. *When does it work?* Second, we may want to know if a particular instructional method is effective for certain kinds of learners, certain kinds of instructional objectives, or certain kinds of learning environments. For example, we can carry out the same comparisons of lectures separately for higher-performing students and lower-performing students, in order to see if the effects of smiling and gesturing are the same for different kinds of learners.
3. *How does it work?* Third, we may want to know what is going on in the learner's mind during learning, that is, what are the mechanisms by which the instructional method causes its effect. For example, we can ask learners to describe what is going on in their minds as they listen to the lecture in which the lecturer smiles and gestures, or we can ask them to fill out a questionnaire or respond to an interview about what they were doing during learning.

Three Types of Questions about Instructional Effectiveness			
Question	**Issue**	**Example**	**Method**
What works?	Does an instructional method cause learning?	Do students learn better if I smile and gesture during my lecture than if I do not?	Experimental comparison
When does it work?	Does an instruction method work better for certain kinds of learners, instructional objectives, or learning environments?	Are the effects of smiling and gesturing during my lecture stronger for women or men?	Factorial experimental comparison
How does it work?	What are the mechanisms underlying the effectiveness of the method?	Why do people learn better from my lecture if I smile and gesture?	Observational analysis, questionnaire, or interview

What Works? Using Randomized Controlled Experiments

How can we tell if an instructional method works? *Experimental comparisons* are the most powerful way to determine whether an instructional manipulation caused a change in the learner's knowledge. In short, when your goal is to determine whether an instructional method had an effect on learning outcomes, the ideal choice is to conduct an experimental comparison. An experimental comparison (also called a *randomized controlled experiment*, or simply an *experiment*) has three main features: *experimental control, random assignment,* and *appropriate measures.*

Three Features of Experiments		
Feature	**Definition**	**Example**
Experimental control	Experimental and control groups receive identical treatment in all respects except for one feature (i.e., the instructional treatment).	One group reads a textbook lesson (control group) and another reads the same lesson with keywords highlighted in bold font.
Random assignment	The learners are randomly assigned to groups (or treatment conditions).	For 50 students, 25 receive a control lesson and 25 receive an experimental lesson, in a selection process based on chance.
Appropriate measures	For each group the mean (M), standard deviation (SD), and sample size (n) are reported for a relevant measure of learning.	On a 20-item comprehension test, the 25 students in the experimental group score higher ($M = 15$, $SD = 3$) than the 25 students in the control group ($M = 12$, $SD = 3$).

To conduct an experimental comparison, first you create a control lesson (such as a textbook chapter on ocean waves) and then alter one feature in the lesson to create a treatment lesson (such as the same lesson with keywords highlighted in bold font). You have maintained experimental control in that all of the features in your two lessons are identical except the one that you are intentionally manipulating. Next, you identify a sample of learners and randomly choose who will receive the control lesson and who will receive the treatment lesson. In this way, you have fulfilled the requirement of random assignment. Finally, you give all learners a test that taps understanding of the material; from the learners' scores you can compute the mean score and standard deviation of each group. In this way you have fulfilled the requirement of appropriate measures.

These definitions and examples assume that you will have two different groups (called a *between subjects design*), but it is also possible to give the control lesson and treatment lesson to the same learners, in which case you have two different treatment conditions rather than two different groups (called a *within subjects design*). Most experimental comparisons of instructional methods use between subjects designs.

In the following box, let's see if these requirements—experimental control, random assignment, and appropriate measures—make sense to you.

Place a check mark next to each scenario that meets the requirements of an experimental comparison:

____ We create a new instructional method for teaching arithmetic. After administering a pretest, we give an experimental lesson (using our new instructional method) to a group of students and then administer a posttest. The students show a large increase from pretest to posttest, so we conclude the instructional method is effective.

____ We create a new instructional method for teaching arithmetic. We give the experimental treatment using our new instructional method (in this case discussion) to one group of students while giving another group of students the standard treatment that the teacher usually uses (in this case, lecture). On a posttest, the experimental group outperforms the standard group, so we conclude that the new instructional method is effective.

____ We create a new instructional method for teaching arithmetic. We ask Ms. Apple at Sunny Valley School to administer a lesson that incorporates the instructional method in her classroom, and we ask Mr. Prune in Frostbite Mountain School to administer the same lesson but without the instructional method in his classroom. On a posttest, Ms. Apple's students outperform Mr. Prune's students, so we conclude that the instructional method is effective.

____ We create a new instructional method for teaching arithmetic. In a classroom of 30 students, we randomly choose 15 to receive the experimental lesson and 15 to receive a control lesson that is identical except for the instructional method. We ask students to rate how much they learned on a scale from 1 to 10. Students in the experimental group report that they learned more than students in the control group, so we conclude that the instructional method is effective.

If you did not check any of the boxes, you either understand how experimental comparisons work or you forgot to bring your pencil. The first two scenarios lack experimental control (although the second is better controlled than the first), the third lacks random assignment (although you may be able to use statistical techniques to equalize the groups), and the fourth lacks appropriate measures. As you can see, there are many ways to falter when you try to answer the question, "What works?"

In *Estimating Causal Effects*, commissioned by the American Educational Research Association, the consensus among educational researchers is that experiments should be used to assess *instructional effects*:

> When correctly implemented, the randomized controlled experiment is the most powerful design for detecting treatment effects. (p. 11)

When Does It Work? Using Factorial Experiments

Asking what works is a good first step but it provides only a somewhat gross indication of instructional effectiveness. For example, suppose that based on several experimental comparisons, researchers have found that students learn better from a lecture when the lecturer smiles and gestures. The theoretical rationale is that students may feel more personally involved in the lecture and therefore try harder to understand what the lecturer is saying. An important next step is to determine whether there are any boundary conditions for the instructional principle; that is, we want to know for whom, for what kind of material, and for what kind of learning situation does the principle apply or not apply. To address this question, we can conduct an experiment in which we randomly assign students to a lecture in which the lecturer smiles and gestures or an otherwise identical lecture in which the lecturer does not smile or gesture. We also note whether students sat in the front half or back half of the class. This is a *factorial experiment* because there are multiple factors—in this case, treatment group is one factor and type of student is another factor. The following table shows a possible pattern of results on a subsequent test (based on percent correct).

A Factorial Comparison Using a Quasi-Experiment		
	Type of Student	
Treatment Group	**Students Who Sat in Front**	**Students Who Sat in Back**
Lecture with smiles and gestures	80%	60%
Lecture with no smiles or gestures	60%	60%

In this case, the instructional treatment—smiling and gesturing—has a substantial effect for students who sat at the front of the class but not for students who sat in back. Thus, we have identified an important boundary condition for the smiling-and-gesturing effect, that is, it works mainly for students who sit in the front of the room. This is a *quasi-experiment* because we did not randomly assign students to groups—that is, we let students sit wherever they wished. If we randomly assign students to seats and to their lecture group, then we have an experiment (rather than a quasi-experiment). Identifying boundary conditions for instructional effects is an important goal of assessment.

How Does It Work? Using Observational Analysis

In addition to determining which instructional treatments work and when they work, the next step is to determine how they work. For example, why would smiling and gesturing during a lecture cause students to learn more? A useful assessment technique in answering such questions is *observational analysis,* in which we observe and describe what people do during the learning episode. Observational analysis sometimes involves classifying our observations into categories based on a scoring rubric. For example, as shown in the following box, we may carefully observe a student during the lecture every 15 seconds and record what the student is doing—engaging in on-task activity (such as looking at the instructor, looking at the screen, or writing notes) or engaging in off-task activity (such as looking elsewhere, texting, doodling, or checking email).

A Rubric for Classroom Observation

Every 15 seconds observe the learner and record:

____ On task (looking at instructor, looking at screen, writing notes)
____ Off task (texting, checking email, doodling, looking elsewhere)

Suppose students in the smiling-and-gesturing group spend more time on on-task activities such as taking notes whereas students in the control group spend more time engaged in off-task activities. This would indicate that smiling and gesturing causes students to work harder. Also, let's look at the notes taken by students in the two groups. We classify each idea in the notes as a basic fact or a deeper implication. Suppose we find that students in the smiling-and-gesturing group have more deep ideas in their notes, whereas students in the control group have more basic information. Taken together, these observational analyses suggest that smiling and gesturing cause the learner to try harder.

A related technique is to use an interview or questionnaire, in which we ask learners to describe what they were thinking or doing as they learned. For example, after the lesson we might ask the simple question following.

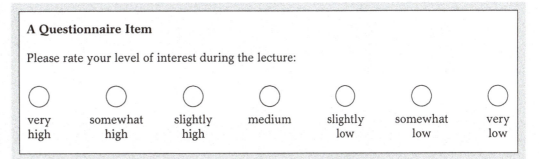

A Questionnaire Item

Please rate your level of interest during the lecture:

| very high | somewhat high | slightly high | medium | slightly low | somewhat low | very low |

If students in the smiling-and-gesturing group give higher ratings than students in the control group, this supports the idea that our instructional treatment works because it causes learners to try harder. Overall, observing what learners do (and say they do) provides important evidence about how instruction works.

A Closer Look at Experiments

Suppose you conducted an experimental comparison that produced the following results, in which the treatment group (also called an *experimental group*) averaged a score of 85 on a transfer test whereas the control group averaged a score of 80, with both groups having a standard deviation of 10.

Results of an Experimental Comparison

Group	Mean (*M*)	Standard Deviation (*SD*)	Sample Size (*n*)
Treatment	85	10	30
Control	80	10	30

How can we tell if the difference is practically important for education? One useful way to assess the practical importance of an experimental comparison is to compute the effect size—as described next.

Using Effect Size to Assess Instructional Effects

Effect size is a measure of the strength of an effect. It provides a common metric for evaluating instructional effectiveness—the number of standard deviations of improvement (or harm) caused by the instructional method as compared to a control group. Based on Jacob Cohen's classic book *Statistical Power Analysis for the Behavioral Sciences*, we can compute effect size (called *d*) by subtracting the mean score of the control group from the mean score of the treatment group and dividing by the pooled standard deviation.

$$\text{effect size} = \frac{\text{mean of treatment group} - \text{mean of control group}}{\text{pooled standard deviation of both groups}}$$

If we return to the experimental comparison shown at the top of the page, the effect size is (85 – 80)/10 or .5.

$$\text{effect size} = \frac{85 - 80}{10} = .5$$

This means that the experimental group scored one-half standard deviation higher than the control group.

Some researchers use other measures of effect size, such as eta squared (η^2), but the goal of all effect size measures is the same—to determine the strength of the effect. As shown in the following chart, according to Jacob Cohen, an effect size of $d = .5$ is considered a medium effect.

Effect Size (*d*)	Strength
Less than .2	Negligible
.2	Small
.5	Medium
.8 or greater	Large

What's wrong with these guidelines? As noted by Jacob Cohen and others, even a small effect can turn out to be very important depending on the situation being studied. For example, Robert Rosenthal and colleagues describe a study comparing the heart attack rate of people who were assigned to either taking an aspirin or a placebo every other day. Although the effect size for aspirin taking was very small, it resulted in 3.4% fewer people getting heart attacks—an effect that clearly is important.

Using Effect Size in Meta-Analyses

Replication refers to conducting the same experimental comparison over again, perhaps with different lesson content, kinds of students, or learning venues. Replication of experimental comparisons is useful to determine how far the effect can generalize beyond the original experiment. When a large number of experiments making the same treatment-control comparison are conducted, it is possible to compute the average effect size. This process of computing average effect size over many experimental comparisons is called *meta-analysis*. In a meta-analysis, it is also possible to determine whether large effect sizes occur mainly for certain kinds of learners, certain kinds of instructional objectives, or certain kinds of learning environments.

For example, consider the following meta-analysis of 40 experimental comparisons. Instructional method 1 had a medium-to-large effect for low knowledge learners (based on 12 comparisons) but no effect for high knowledge learners (based on 10 comparisons). In contrast, instructional method 2 had a medium effect on high knowledge learners (based on 8 comparisons) but no effect on low knowledge learners (based on 10 comparisons). As you can see, as evidence begins to accumulate, you can tell what works and the conditions under which it works. Method 1 appears to be more effective for low knowledge learners whereas method 2 appears to be more effective for high knowledge learners.

A Hypothetical Meta-Analysis

	Type of Learner			
	High Prior Knowledge		Low Prior Knowledge	
Instructional Method	Mean *d*	Number	Mean *d*	Number
Method 1	.1	10	.7	12
Method 2	.5	8	.0	10

Six Reasons for No Difference between the Treatment and Control Groups

Suppose you have devised a new instructional method for teaching foreign language vocabulary. You conduct a randomized controlled experiment (hereafter called an *experiment*), but your treatment group does not perform significantly better than the control group on the posttest. Why was there no significant difference? The following table explores six possible reasons for finding no difference between the treatment group and control group in an experiment.

Why Is There No Difference between the Treatment Group and the Control Group?		
Reason	**Example**	**Solution**
Treatment effectiveness	The treatment is not effective.	Conclude that the method does not work.
Inadequate sample size	There are not enough learners in each group.	Increase sample size.
Dependent measure insensitivity	The dependent measure(s) were not sensitive enough to detect differences in learning outcomes.	Use more appropriate measures.
Treatment fidelity	The treatment and control groups were not different enough from each other.	Implement more extreme treatments.
Learner insensitivity	The learners were not sensitive enough to the treatment.	Choose more appropriate learners.
Confounding variables	The treatment and control groups differ on an important variable.	Statistically control for the confounding variable.

The most straightforward reason for finding no effect is that your treatment is not effective. This is the conclusion you must draw—at least for the time being—if the groups do not differ significantly on the dependent measure. However, the statistical tests we typically use are designed to minimize the chances that you will conclude there is an effect when there is not (*type I error*), and may exaggerate the chances that you conclude there is no effect when there really is one (*type II error*). As shown in the following table, educational researchers put a great value on avoiding type I errors (by setting it to $p < .05$ in most experiments), which increases the chances of committing type II errors.

Two Types of Statistical Error

Type	Description	Explanation
Type I error	Concluding there is an effect when there is not	$p < .05$ means there is less than a 5% chance of committing a type 1 error
Type II error	Concluding there is not an effect when there is	$p < .05$ does not refer to type 2 error, but the chances of type 2 error may be far greater than 5%

Let's consider some other reasons for finding no significant difference between the control and experimental groups even though your instructional method can work. Perhaps the most common problem is that there are not enough learners in each group. According to a *statistical power analysis* (based on .80 strength) as suggested by Jacob Cohen, if there is a strong effect size ($d = .8$) you would need 26 learners in each group, if there is a medium effect size ($d = .5$) you would need 64 learners in each group, and if there is a small effect size ($d = .2$) you would need 393 learners in each group. When you have 10 or 12 learners in each group, for example, you may not have enough power to adequately test whether your instructional method works. This problem is exacerbated when the learners within each group are quite different from each other.

Number of Learners Needed in Each Group to Achieve Adequate Statistical Power

Expected Effect Size	Number of Learners Needed in Each Group
Strong ($d = .8$)	26
Medium ($d = .5$)	64
Small ($d = .2$)	393

Another common reason for no significant difference is that the dependent measure does not adequately tap the learning outcome. Your test needs to meet the criteria for a useful test (which are listed on page 96). Designing appropriate dependent measures can be the most challenging aspect of experimental research, so assessment of learning outcomes plays a central role in applying the science of learning.

Another potential reason for finding no significant difference is that the experimental treatment is not strong enough—that is, the experimental treatment is too similar to the control treatment—or the experimental and control treatments are not administered consistently—for example, a teacher in the control group might supplement instruction with material from the experimental group on her own initiative. Another possible reason is that the treatments are not appropriate for the learners; for example, an outstanding method for teaching calculus probably will not have a strong positive effect if used with students who have not mastered arithmetic. Finally, you need to make sure learners are randomly assigned to the experimental and control groups so there are no confounds.

How to Assess Learning Outcomes

One of the most important and challenging tasks in applying the science of learning is developing useful measures of learning outcomes. In particular, we need ways of measuring for understanding, which are explored in this section and the next one.

Two Ways to Measure Learning Outcomes

Two classic methods for measuring learning outcomes are *retention tests,* such as asking a learner to recall or recognize what was learned, and *transfer tests,* such as asking a learner to use what was learned in a new situation. Retention tests focus on remembering and are the most commonly used form of assessment, whereas transfer tests focus on understanding, which is a commonly stated goal of education. I focus mainly on transfer tests in this book because I am most interested in promoting understanding (in addition to remembering).

Two Ways to Measure Learning Outcomes			
Type of Test	**Goal of Test**	**Definition**	**Example**
Retention	Remembering	Recall or recognize the presented material	Please write down all you remember about the device described in the lesson.
Transfer	Understanding	Evaluate or use the material in a new situation	How would you improve the device you just learned about to make it more effective?

How much transfer should be used in tests? Retention tests involve no transfer, requiring only the application of the just learned principle or method to situations that are identical or very similar to those in the instruction. Near transfer involves asking learners to solve problems that require applying the newly learned principle or method in new situations. Far transfer involves asking learners to solve problems that require inventing a new principle or method. For example, if you had just learned how to solve two-column subtraction problems such as $54 - 35 =$ ___, then retention would involve solving problems like $64 - 45 =$ ___, near transfer would involve solving problems like $354 - 135 =$ ___, and far transfer would involve solving problems like $54 - x = 19$.

Three Degrees of Transfer in Test Problems		
Degree	**Description**	**Example**
Retention	Solve same or very similar problem	After learning to solve two-column subtraction problems, the test involves more two-column subtraction problems.
Near transfer	Solve new problem that requires applying the same principle or method in a new situation	After learning to solve two-column subtraction problems, the test involves three-column subtraction problems.
Far transfer	Solve new problem that requires applying a new principle or method in a new situation	After learning to solve two-column subtraction problems, the test involves solving equations requiring subtraction.

In my own research, the most sensitive transfer test problems involve near transfer, so I focus on near transfer measures when the assessment goal is to measure learner understanding of the material in the lesson.

Three Kinds of Learning Outcomes

Based on learner performance on retention and transfer tests we can identify three types of learning outcome—*no learning,* which is indicated by poor performance on retention and transfer tests; *rote learning,* which is indicated by good retention and poor transfer performance; and *meaningful learning,* which is indicated by good performance on retention and transfer.

Three Kinds of Learning Outcomes			
Learning Outcome	**Cognitive Description**	**Retention Test Score**	**Transfer Test Score**
No learning	No knowledge	Poor	Poor
Rote learning	Fragmented knowledge	Good	Poor
Meaningful learning	Integrated knowledge	Good	Good

As you can see in the table, the main difference between meaningful and rote learning is indicated by transfer test performance. Thus, I am particularly interested in transfer tests as important indicators of learning outcomes.

In addition to using quantitative methods of assessing learning outcomes, we can also use qualitative methods such as interviewing learners after or during learning, observing students during learning (including examining their log files in a computer-based learning environment), or interacting with them during learning to determine how much guidance they need. Qualitative descriptions can add richness to the description of learning outcomes, and can help elucidate the underlying learning processes.

A Closer Look at Meaningful versus Rote Learning: Wertheimer's Parallelogram Lesson

The distinction between rote and meaningful learning has a long history in psychology and education, such as described by the famous Gestalt psychologist Max Wertheimer in his classic book, *Productive Thinking*. As an example of the distinction between rote and meaningful learning, Wertheimer asks you to suppose you wanted to teach students how to find the area of parallelogram, such as shown in the following figure.

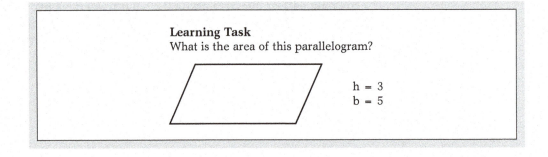

Learning Task
What is the area of this parallelogram?

h = 3
b = 5

A *rote learning* approach is to show students the procedure for solving parallelogram problems, illustrated on the left in the following figure. This is a rote approach because the learner is told what to do without explaining why to do it. A *meaningful learning* approach— shown in the following figure on the right—is to allow students to cut a triangle from one end of a paper parallelogram and tape it to the other end to form a rectangle. In this way the learner can experience what Wertheimer calls *structural insight*—in this case, seeing that a parallelogram is a rectangle in disguise. Assuming the learner already knows how to find the area of a rectangle, this insight is all that is needed to solve the problem.

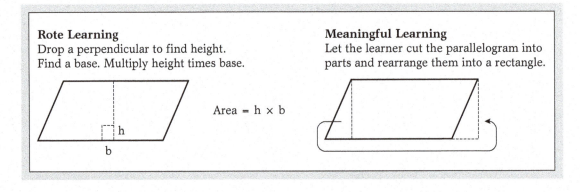

Rote Learning
Drop a perpendicular to find height.
Find a base. Multiply height times base.

Area = h × b

h
b

Meaningful Learning
Let the learner cut the parallelogram into parts and rearrange them into a rectangle.

According to Wertheimer, students taught by either the rote method or the meaningful method are able to solve retention problems—that is, problems in which they are asked to find the area of parallelogram like the one in the lesson. For example, they could be asked to solve a problem identical to the "Learning Task" but with $h = 4$ and $b = 6$.

However, what happens when we give them transfer problems such as shown in the next illustration? For example, rote learners may drop a perpendicular for the parallelogram (on the left side) and then look confused and say, "We haven't had this yet." In contrast, meaningful learners are able to mentally rearrange the shape in a rectangle and then solve the problem. As you can see, transfer test performance is the dependent measure that distinguishes meaningful and rote learning outcomes.

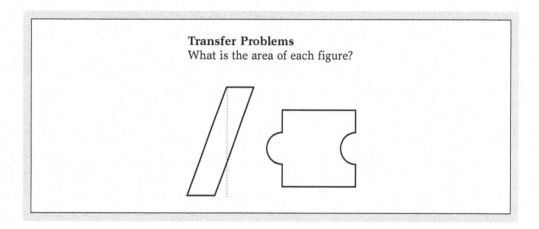

Transfer Problems
What is the area of each figure?

Max Wertheimer was one of the first researchers to show the importance of transfer tests—in addition to retention tests—for evaluating learning outcomes. When your goal is to assess the learner's understanding of the material in a lesson, appropriate assessment should include transfer items. The taxonomy of instructional objectives shown on page 61 provides examples of ways to test for transfer that go beyond simple retention.

A Closer Look at Assessment of Learning Outcomes: How Much or What Kind?

In measuring learning outcomes, we can take a *how much* approach or a *what kind* approach, as summarized in the following table. The most common approach is to focus on how much is learned, such as indicated by percent correct or number correct on a test. This approach is based on the knowledge acquisition metaphor (as described on page 22), in which learning is viewed as filling up an empty container. In some cases, the *how much* approach may be appropriate, such as when your instructional objective is to help the learner attain a certain level of test performance. In contrast, consider the *what kind* approach, in which we seek to describe the structure of the learner's knowledge. This approach is based on the knowledge construction metaphor (as described on pages 22–23), in which learning is viewed as building a knowledge representation. The *what kind* approach can provide more specific information concerning how to adjust instruction, because it provides a clearer description of what the learner knows.

Two Approaches to Assessment of Learning Outcomes		
Approach	**Description**	**Example**
How much	Determine how much is learned	You correctly solved 50% of the subtraction problems.
What kind	Determine what is learned	Your subtraction procedure has the smaller-from-larger bug.

Rationale for the *What Kind* Approach: The Case for Error Analysis

Consider Sal's performance on the following subtraction problems:

54 – 33 = 21

63 – 29 = 46

67 – 15 = 52

65 – 16 = 51

If we take a *how much* approach to assessment, we could say that Sal scored at 50%. The instructional implications are that Sal needs more instruction, but the *how much* approach does not give us much specific guidance about what to do. In contrast, if we take a *what kind* approach, we might notice that Sal's subtraction procedure has what John Sealy Brown and

Richard Burton call a *smaller-from-larger bug*—that is, for each column Sal simply subtracts the smaller number from the larger number. In short, Sal appears to be correctly applying an incorrect procedure. If we know which step is wrong, we can design instruction aimed at repairing Sal's knowledge. This version of the *what kind* approach can be called *error analysis* because it helps to pinpoint specific misconceptions in people's knowledge.

Rationale for the *What Kind* Approach: The Case for Multileveled Posttests

As another example, suppose we teach some students how to solve binomial probability problems using a deductive method—which emphasizes how to compute correct answers using the formula—and we teach other students using an inductive method—which emphasizes how the formula is related to familiar concepts. On a subsequent posttest, the deductive group outperforms the inductive group on computing answers to binomial probability problems—which is a retention test. If we take a *how much* approach and stop with an assessment based only on a retention test, we might conclude that the deductive group learned more than the inductive group. However, when James Greeno and I conducted this comparison, we also included transfer test questions, such as unsolvable problems that required students to answer that the problems could not be solved. The inductive group outperformed the deductive group on the transfer items, whereas the deductive group outperformed the inductive group on the retention items. When we used a *multileveled posttest*—involving both retention and transfer items—we found evidence not that one group learned more than the other but rather that the groups had structurally different learning outcomes. Thus, one way to implement a *what kind* approach is to conduct multileveled posttests, as shown in the following figure.

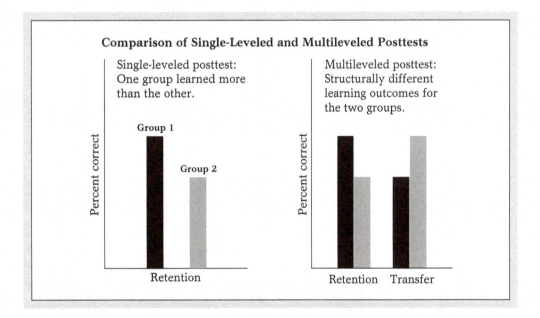

Comparison of Single-Leveled and Multileveled Posttests

Single-leveled posttest: One group learned more than the other.

Multileveled posttest: Structurally different learning outcomes for the two groups.

Overall, the rationale for the *what kind* approach—such as using error analysis or multileveled posttests—is that it provides more useful information concerning what was learned and therefore can be more helpful in informing instructional decisions.

Broadening the Domain of Assessment

So far, we have focused mainly on assessment of learning outcomes, but there are other domains of assessment that are relevant to our task of applying the science of learning. The following table lists some additional domains of assessment.

What Else to Assess		
Type	**Source(s)**	**Examples**
Demographic characteristics	Survey, records	Age, sex, ethnicity, parents' education levels
Cognitive characteristics	Survey, test, observation	Learning ability, cognitive abilities, academic achievement
Motivational characteristics	Survey, observation	Motivational goals, learning beliefs, attributions
Personality characteristics	Survey, observation	Personality traits
Task-specific characteristics	Survey, test, observation	Interest, task-specific motivation, prior knowledge
Learning processes	Survey, observation	Strategies, effort, activities, self-monitoring

Broadening the Domain of Assessment to Determine When Instructional Methods Work

Assessment of learning outcomes with tests is useful for determining "What works?" because we can compare the learning outcomes (based on test performance) of experimental and control groups. However, when we want to address the question of "When does it work?" (or "For whom does it work?"), it may be useful to examine the learners' demographic, cognitive, motivational, personality, task-specific, and learning process characteristics.

A test is a printed, online, or concrete activity in which the learner is asked to answer questions, solve problems, or perform tasks. For example, if you wanted to assess someone's prior knowledge in arithmetic you could give them a three-minute arithmetic test containing 60 arithmetic problems, such as $55 \times 2 =$ ___.

An observation involves recording the learner's activity during a task. For example, to assess learning ability, you could give learners an online lesson and record how many times they pressed the help button in order to master the material. To assess their motivation to learn, you could record whether they choose to continue on a task when given the opportunity to do so.

A survey is a printed questionnaire, online questionnaire, or spoken interview used for soliciting information about the learner's characteristics. For example, to determine *demographic characteristics* such as the learner's age we can use a survey (i.e., a printed questionnaire or spoken interview) in which the learner is asked to provide information, such as "Your age: ___".

Broadening the Domain of Assessment to Determine How Instructional Methods Work

Assessment of learning outcomes is useful for determining "What works?" (i.e., Does a particular instructional method improve learning outcomes?) but you may also want to know "How does it work?" (i.e., How does a particular instructional method improve learning outcomes?). In this situation, you want to know what is going on during the learning process, so it may be useful for you to observe the learner's behavior during learning (such as the amount of time the learner is "off task" during a PowerPoint presentation, the quality of notes taken during a lecture, or the kinds of websites visited during an online writing task). Alternatively, it may be useful to ask learners to describe their thought processes either after learning (as a retrospective survey or interview) or during learning (as a thinking aloud activity or survey). From this information, you can infer the learner's cognitive processing during learning—such as the degree to which the learner was cognitively engaged in learning.

For example, Krista DeLeeuw and I examined three ways to assess the learner's cognitive load during learning from a multimedia lesson: a secondary task, an effort rating during learning, and a difficulty rating after learning. For the secondary task, the learner was asked to press the space bar if the background color on the screen changed from pink to black, with longer response times indicating higher levels of cognitive load. For the effort rating, at various points in the lesson, the learner was asked to "rate your level of mental effort on this part of the lesson" on a nine-point scale from "extremely low mental effort" to "extremely high mental effort." For the difficulty rating, after the lesson was over, the learner was asked to indicate "how difficult was the lesson" on a nine-point scale ranging from "extremely easy" to "extremely difficult." For example, try the following questionnaire. Do you think you are able to give an accurate assessment?

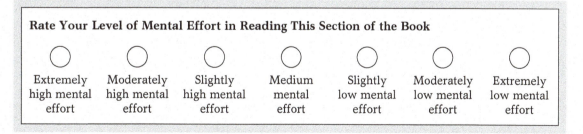

Rate Your Level of Mental Effort in Reading This Section of the Book

| Extremely high mental effort | Moderately high mental effort | Slightly high mental effort | Medium mental effort | Slightly low mental effort | Moderately low mental effort | Extremely low mental effort |

The creation of useful assessment instruments that broaden the domain of assessment is a major challenge of educational research.

A Closer Look at Broadening the Domain of Assessment: Attribute Treatment Interactions

What Is an Attribute Treatment Interaction (ATI)?

Suppose you teach a lesson using one instructional method (method A) for some learners and by another instructional method (method B) for other learners, and that within each group you have two different kinds of learners (type 1 and type 2). The following graphs show three possible patterns of performance on a posttest.

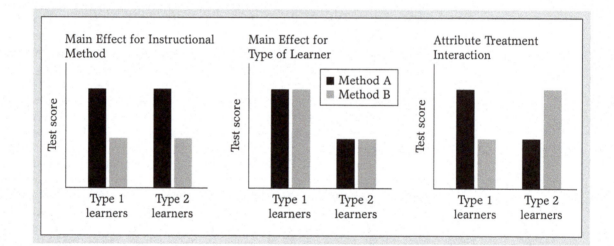

The results of a posttest could show only a main effect for instructional method, in which for example, students score higher with method A than method B (as shown in the left graph). The results could show only a main effect for type of learner, in which for example, type 1 learners score higher on a posttest than type 2 learners (as shown in the middle graph). Finally, the results could show an interaction, in which for example, method A works best for type 1 learners and method B works best for type 2 learners (as shown in the right graph). This is an *attribute treatment interaction* (or attribute × treatment interaction, or simply, ATI) because the effect of an instructional method depends on the attributes of the learner.

An attribute treatment interaction occurs when the effects of an instructional method depend on the attributes of the learner. In the strictest sense, an ATI occurs when one instructional method is better for one kind of learner and a different instructional method is better for another kind of learner, as shown in the following right-hand graph. This pattern is called a *disordinal interaction* or *interaction with crossover*. In a more lenient sense an ATI occurs when an instructional method is more effective for one kind of learner than another kind of learner (e.g., the difference between methods A and B is strong for type 2 learners but not for type 1 learners), as shown in the left-hand graph. This pattern is called an *ordinal interaction or interaction without crossover.*

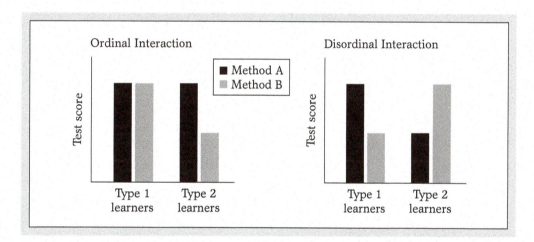

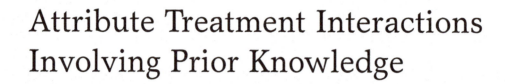

Attribute Treatment Interactions
Involving Prior Knowledge

An important individual differences characteristic is the learner's prior knowledge. If you could know only one characteristic about your students, you would want to find out what they already know about the topic you intend to teach them. For example, suppose your students will be given a lesson on how car brakes work—consisting of printed text and illustrations. In order to assess your students' prior knowledge, you give them a brief survey (or questionnaire) which asks them to indicate on a checklist what they have done involving car mechanics and also to rate their knowledge of car mechanics. Go ahead and complete the following survey.

Survey of Prior Knowledge Concerning Car Mechanics

Please place a check mark next to the things you have done:

____ I have a driver's license.
____ I have put air in a car's tire.
____ I have changed a tire on a car.
____ I have changed oil in a car.
____ I have replaced the brake shoes in a car.

Please place a check mark indicating your knowledge of car mechanics and repair:

____ very much

____
____ average

____
____ very little

To score the survey we can give 1 point for each item you checked on the first checklist and 1 to 5 points on the second item (with 1 for very little and 5 for very much). If you scored higher than the median (which generally is 4), then you are high in prior knowledge, and if you scored below the median, you are low in prior knowledge.

Suppose we ask high and low prior knowledge learners to read a lesson on brakes that is well designed (i.e., the words are placed next to the corresponding illustrations) or poorly designed (i.e., the words are separated from the corresponding illustrations on the page). Suppose low-knowledge learners score higher on a posttest when they receive the well-designed lesson as opposed to the poorly designed lesson, and in contrast, the high-knowledge learners score well with both instructional methods. In the following graph on the left, the low-knowledge learners score high for the well-designed lesson (method A) but low for the poorly designed lesson (method B), whereas the high-knowledge learners score high for both methods. Alternatively, suppose there is a crossover interaction such as shown on the right-hand graph: The low-knowledge learners score higher for the well-designed lesson (method A) than for the poorly designed lesson (method B), whereas the high-knowledge learners score higher on the poorly designed lesson than on the well-designed lesson.

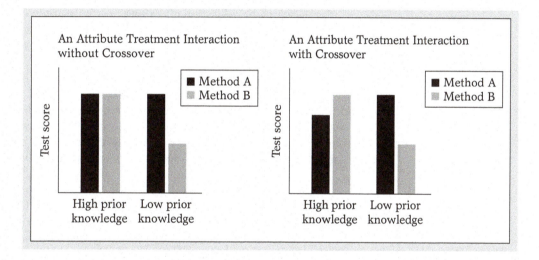

The pattern on the right is an example of what Slava Kalyuga calls the *expertise reversal effect*—instructional methods that are more effective for low-knowledge learners may be less effective for high-knowledge learners. There is some research evidence in support of the expertise reversal effect. In general, low-knowledge learners benefit more from well-structured lessons whereas high-knowledge learners benefit from less structured kinds of instructional methods. An important instructional implication concerns establishing boundary conditions for instructional effects—that is, determining for whom the effects are strongest (such as method A being most effective for low-knowledge learners).

Should we have different instruction methods for different kinds of learners? This is an important research question that is still largely an open question. In spite of several decades of research, for example, Laura Massa and I have shown that there is still not ample evidence to support the claim that verbal learners learn better from words and visual learners learn better with pictures. In short, the best-established ATI concerns prior knowledge, so in searching for effective instructional methods it is worthwhile to note whether they are effective mainly for low-knowledge learners or high-knowledge learners. If you are interested in adapting instruction based on individual differences, you should remember that the most important individual differences dimension is prior knowledge—that is, the knowledge that the learner brings to the learning situation.

What Can Go Wrong with Assessments?

Scenario 1: Professor Mann thinks that using clickers (i.e., hand-held remote controls) in his large lecture class may improve learning. In one section of his class he does not use clickers but in another section he asks students to use clickers to register votes on various questions posed during class. At the end of the course, he hands out a survey in which he asks students to rate how much they liked the course. Students give overwhelmingly higher ratings in the clicker group than in the no-clicker group, so Professor Mann concludes that clickers are a big success.

What's wrong with this scenario? The problem is that liking is not the same as learning. Even though students may like an instructional method, their fondness for the method does not translate necessarily into improvements in learning outcomes. If your instructional goal is to promote learning, then you should be careful to include relevant measures of learning outcome. You can use measures of liking to help answer questions about how an instructional method works but not to determine whether it works.

Scenario 2: In Ms. Manning's 12th grade mathematics class, students have been learning about how to solve binomial probability problems. To assess how well the students are learning, she asks them to fill out a questionnaire in which they rate how well they know the material. Students overwhelmingly claim to know the material very well, so Ms. Manning concludes that her teaching has been successful.

What's wrong with scenario 2? The problem is that students may lack the self-awareness to be able to gage their own learning. They may think they are working hard and learning a lot, when in fact that are not learning much at all. What is needed is a more valid test of learning outcome, such as asking students to solve binomial probability problems.

Scenario 3: A researcher is interested in whether a two-week American history course improves students' knowledge of American history. As a pretest, students are asked to answer several essay questions about American history and as a posttest students are asked to answer several more essay questions about American history. The researcher examines the pretest-to-posttest gain in answer quality for students who were assigned to take the program and those who were not.

Overall, the problem with scenario 3 is that the pretest may serve as an instructional activity. The act of taking the pretest may help students learn. If the instructional effect of pretesting is strong, it can wash out the effects of instructional treatment used in the study. This would be a detriment to your assessment efforts, but would be a good outcome if your goal is to promote learning.

These three assessment malfunctions are summarized in the following table. As you can see, it is important to use assessment instruments that assess what you intend them to assess and that are as unobtrusive as possible.

Three Ways for Assessments to Go Wrong	
Description	**Example**
Measuring the wrong variable	Measuring liking rather than learning
Using the wrong instrument	Focusing on self-rating of learning rather than performance
Overtesting	Using a learning pretest that overshadows the treatment

Pages 93–94

Anderson, L. W., Krathwohl, D. R., Airasian, P. W., Cruikshank, K. A., Mayer, R. E., Pintrich, P. R., Raths, J., & Wittrock, M. C. (2001). *A taxonomy for learning, teaching, and assessing: A revision of Bloom's taxonomy of educational objectives.* New York: Longman.

A framework for creating instructional objectives based on advances in the science of learning, written by a team of experts in learning, instruction, and assessment.

Pages 95–97

American Educational Research Association, American Psychological Association, and National Council on Measurement in Education (1999). *Standards for educational and psychological testing.* Washington, DC: American Educational Research Association.

A careful analysis of how to design tests, commissioned by the American Educational Research Association, the American Psychological Association, and the National Council on Measurement in Education.

Pellegrino, J. W., Chudowsky, N., & Glaser, R. (Eds.). (2001). *Knowing what students know: The science and design of assessment.* Washington, DC: National Academy Press.

A careful analysis of how to assess learning outcomes, commissioned by the National Research Council and written by leading assessment researchers.

Pages 98–103

Schneider, B., Carnoy, M., Kilpatrick, J., Schmidt, W. H., & Shavelson, R. J. (2005). *Estimating causal effects: Using experimental and observational designs.* Washington, DC: American Educational Research Association.

A careful analysis of how to determine whether an instructional method causes learning.

Pages 104–107

Cohen, J. (1988). *Statistical power analysis for the behavioral sciences* (2nd ed.). Hillsdale, NJ: Erlbaum.

A classic description of how to compute and use effect size.

Rosenthal, R., Rosnow, R. L., & Rubin, D. B. (2000). *Contrasts and effect sizes in the behavioral sciences.* New York: Cambridge University Press.

An excellent resource for measuring effect size.

Pages 112–115

Brown, J. S., & Burton, R. R. (1978). Diagnostic models for procedural bugs in basic arithmetic skills. *Cognitive Science, 2,* 155–192.

A classic study showing the benefits of error analysis.

Mayer, R. E., & Greeno, J. G. (1972). Structural differences between learning outcomes produced by different instructional methods. *Journal of Educational Psychology, 63,* 165–173.

A classic study showing the benefits of multileveled posttests.

Wertheimer, M. (1959). *Productive thinking.* New York: Harper & Row.

A classic book on how to promote meaningful learning, by a leading Gestalt psychologist.

Pages 116–117

DeLeeuw, K. E., & Mayer, R. E. (2008). A comparison of three measures of cognitive load: Evidence for separable measures of intrinsic, extraneous, and germane load. *Journal of Educational Psychology, 100,* 223–234.

A study comparing multiple measures of cognitive load during learning.

Pages 118–121

Cronbach, L. J., & Snow, R. E. (1977). *Aptitudes and instructional methods.* New York: Irvington.

An overview of research on aptitude treatment interactions.

Kalyuga, S. (2005). Prior knowledge principle in multimedia learning. In R. E. Mayer (Ed.), *The Cambridge handbook of multimedia learning* (pp. 325–338). New York: Cambridge University Press.

A summary of research on the expertise reversal effect.

Massa, L. J., & Mayer, R. E. (2006). Testing the ATI hypothesis: Should multimedia instruction accommodate verbalizer–visualizer cognitive style? *Learning and Individual Differences, 16,* 321–338.

An experimental search for attribute treatment interactions (ATIs).

Pages 122–123

Johnson, C. I., & Mayer, R. E. (2009). A testing effect with multimedia learning. *Journal of Educational Psychology, 101,* 621–629.

An example of how the testing effect applies in educational settings.

E P I L O G U E

The task of applying the science of learning to education can enrich both education (which seeks effective instruction for helping people to learn) and the learning sciences (which seek to create accurate accounts of how people learn). For more than 100 years, educators have sought to base instructional practice on research evidence and evidence-based theory—a goal that is now increasingly within reach thanks to advances in our understanding of how learning works (i.e., the science of learning). Similarly, for more than 100 years, learning scientists have sought to develop authentic theories of how learning works—a goal that is now increasingly within reach thanks to the challenges of producing effective instruction in real settings (i.e., the science of instruction). Applying the science of learning involves two overlapping goals—the applied goal of contributing to educational practice (i.e., the science of instruction) and the basic research goal of contributing to learning theory (i.e., the science of learning). Rather than seeing basic and applied research as opposite poles on a continuum, progress can be made by viewing them as two overlapping goals that mutually reinforce each other. In short, applying the science of learning is an example of what can be called *use-inspired basic research.* Applying the science of learning requires an understanding of how learning works, how instruction works, and how assessment works. In taking a scientific approach to learning, instruction, and assessment, our goal is to base conclusions on research evidence rather than on opinion, fads, or ideology.

Science of Learning

The science of learning is the scientific study of how people learn. Three major principles derived from this study are that people have separate channels for processing verbal and visual information (dual channels principle), people can process only a small amount of information in each channel at any one time (limited capacity principle), and meaningful learning occurs when learners engage in appropriate cognitive processing during learning (active processing principle). Learning takes place in an information processing system that consists of sensory memory, working memory, and long-term memory, and depends on the cognitive processes of selecting, organizing, and integrating. Meaningful learning occurs when the learner attends to relevant information in the lesson entering from sensory memory (selecting), mentally organizes the selected material into a coherent representation in working memory (organizing), and integrates the incoming material with other representations and relevant prior knowledge from long-term memory (integrating). Any complete theory of learning must also account for the roles of motivation, metacognition, and individual differences.

Science of Instruction

The science of instruction is the scientific study of how to help people learn. Instructional design of lessons should begin with a clear specification of the instructional objective—that is, a description of the desired knowledge change in the learner. Five kinds of knowledge found in instructional objectives are facts, concepts, procedures, strategies, and beliefs; six kinds of cognitive processes in instructional objectives are to remember, understand, apply, analyze, evaluate, and create.

The demands on the limited processing capacity in working memory include extraneous processing (i.e., cognitive processing that does not support the instructional objective, usually caused by poor instructional presentation), essential processing (i.e., cognitive processing aimed at representing the essential material, caused by the inherent complexity of the material), and generative processing (i.e., cognitive processing aimed at deep understanding of the presented material, caused by the learner's motivation to learn). The major challenge of instructional designers is to create lessons that minimize extraneous processing, manage essential processing, and foster generative processing. The science of instruction has yielded evidence-based principles for how to construct effective lessons based on these challenges.

Science of Assessment

The science of assessment is the scientific study of determining what people know. Assessment of what people know is inferred from assessment of their performance. Three functions of assessment are to determine what students already know before instruction (pre-assessment), to determine what they are learning during instruction (formative assessment), and to give an accounting of what they have learned after instruction (summative assessment). Research on instructional effectiveness seeks to discover which instructional methods are effective (e.g., using experiments), when they are effective (e.g., using factorial experiments), and how they are effective (e.g., using observations and interviews). The core characteristics of experimental comparisons are experimental control, random assignment, and appropriate measures. A practical goal of experimental comparisons is to identify instructional methods that produce large effect sizes under a wide variety of situations. Meaningful learning outcomes are characterized by good retention and good transfer performance, whereas rote learning outcomes are characterized by good retention and poor transfer performance. Transfer is a crucial measure of learning outcomes when the goal is to promote meaningful learning.

Future Directions

My goal in writing this book has been to share with you some of what I think you should know about how learning works, how instruction works, and how assessment works. I have tried to be as concise and focused as possible, which necessitated that I carefully chose what to include. Some related areas that I did not emphasize or even address concern development, social context, cognitive neuroscience, evolution, culture, and policy. Any complete understanding of how to apply the science of learning requires filling in these missing pieces (and more). The key to success in applying the science of learning to education is that we base our conclusions on scientifically rigorous research evidence rather than on opinions, fads, or ideology. In short, the focus of this book is that progress can be made in applying the science of learning by taking a scientific approach to learning, instruction, and assessment.

GLOSSARY and SUBJECT INDEX

active learning The learner's level of cognitive activity during learning rather than the learner's level of behavioral activity during learning. See also *selecting, organizing, integrating*. (pp. 37, 87)

active processing principle A principle from the science of learning that states meaningful learning occurs when learners engage in appropriate cognitive processing during learning (such as attending to relevant material, organizing it into a coherent representation, and integrating it with relevant prior knowledge). See also *dual channels principle, limited capacity principle, selecting, organizing, integrating*. (pp. 30, 33, 35)

analyze An instructional objective that involves breaking material into its constituent parts and determining how the parts relate to one another and to an overall structure or purpose, such as distinguishing between relevant and irrelevant numbers in a probability word problem. See also *remember, understand, apply, evaluate, create*. (p. 61)

anchoring principle An evidence-based principle for fostering generative processing stating that people learn better when material is presented in the context of a familiar situation. See also *multimedia principle, personalization principle, concretizing principle*. (p. 70)

applied research Research that is intended to contribute to practice (e.g., the science of instruction). See also *basic research*. (pp. 10–11)

apply An instructional objective that involves carrying out or using a procedure in a given situation, such as computing the value of binomial probability given values for *N, r,* and *p*. See also *remember, understand, analyze, evaluate, create*. (p. 61)

applying the science of learning Refers to using what is known about how people learn to design instruction that helps people learn. Applying the science of learning involves reciprocal relations among the science of learning, the science of instruction, and the science of assessment. See also *science of learning, science of instruction, science of assessment*. (pp. xi, 6–7, 127)

assessment Determining what a learner has learned (i.e., learning outcome), the way that the learner learned the material (i.e., learning process), or the learner's characteristics related to learning (i.e., learning characteristics). See also *learning, instruction, science of assessment*. (pp. 2, 4–5, 52–63, 93–97)

assimilation to schema Changing incoming information to fit within the structure of existing knowledge. See also *active learning, integrating*. (pp. 28–29)

attention span When presented with a collection of objects, a person's attention span is the largest number of objects he or she can directly detect without having to estimate. See also *memory span, magic number 7*. (p. 32)

attitudinal knowledge See *beliefs*.

attribute treatment interaction (ATI) An interaction that occurs when the effects of an instructional treatment depend on the attributes of the learner, such as when one instructional method is more effective for one kind of learner and another instructional method is more effective for another kind of learner. (pp. 118–121)

Bartlett's assimilation to schema See *assimilation to schema*.

basic research Research that is intended to contribute to theory (e.g., the science of learning). See also *applied research*. (pp. 10–11)

basic research on applied problems Research that is intended to contribute to theory and practice (e.g., to both the science of learning and the science of instruction); referred to as Pasteur's Quadrant. See also *use-inspired basic research*. (p. 11)

belief-based knowledge See *beliefs*.

beliefs Thoughts about learning, such as "I am not good at statistics." See also *facts, concepts, procedures, strategies*. (pp. 14, 17, 40–41, 60)

clustering in free recall The finding that people tend to recall the words in a list by category (such as furniture, parts of the body, professions, etc.) in spite of the presentation order. (p. 47)

cognitive theory of multimedia learning A theory of learning proposed by Richard E. Mayer, which is based on the dual channels principle, limited capacity principle, and active learning principle. According to the theory, meaningful learning occurs when learners select relevant words and select relevant images from the presented material, mentally organize the selected words into a verbal model and mentally organize the selected images into a pictorial model in working memory, and integrate the models with each other and with relevant knowledge from long-term memory. See also *dual channels principle, limited capacity principle, active processing principle, sensory memory, working memory, long-term memory*. (pp. 34–38)

coherence principle An evidence-based principle for reducing extraneous processing stating that people learn better when extraneous material is excluded from a lesson rather than included. See also *signaling principle, spatial contiguity principle, temporal contiguity principle, expectation principle*. (p. 66)

collaborative learning Learning that occurs when a group is given a challenging problem, task, or project to carry out on their own. See also *discovery learning*. (pp. 82, 86)

concepts Categories, schemas, models, or principles, such as knowing that in the number 65, 6 refers to the number of tens. See also *facts, procedures, strategies, beliefs*. (pp. 14, 17, 60)

conceptual knowledge See *concepts*.

concrete advance organizer An instructional technique intended to guide the process of integrating, in which familiar material is presented before a lesson in order to promote deep learning. See also *concrete model, integrating, concretizing principle*. (p. 80)

concrete model An instructional technique intended to guide the process of integrating, in which familiar material is presented during a lesson in order to promote deep learning. See also *concrete advance organizer, integrating, concretizing principle*. (pp. 80–81)

concreteness effect The finding that people can remember concrete words (such as *tree*) better than abstract words (such as *style*). See also *picture superiority effect, dual channels principle*. (pp. 31, 47)

concretizing principle An evidence-based principle for fostering generative processing stating that people learn better when unfamiliar material is related to familiar knowledge. See also *multimedia principle, personalization principle, anchoring principle*. (p. 70)

create An instructional objective that involves putting elements together to form a coherent or functional whole or reorganizing elements into a new pattern or structure, such as planning an essay on the discovery of binomial probability. See also *remember, understand, apply, analyze, evaluate*. (p. 61)

criterion-referenced test A test that tells you whether a specific learning objective has been met, such as whether the learner can accomplish a specified task. See also *norm-referenced test*. (p. 97)

crossover interaction See *disordinal interaction*.

dead-end street A view of the relation between the science of learning and the science of instruction in which basic researchers create learning theories based on contrived learning situations (SOL), which are ignored by applied researchers, and applied researchers create instructional principles that are not grounded in theory (SOI), which are ignored by basic researchers. See also *two-way street, one-way street*. (pp. 8–9)

demographic characteristics Basic information about the learner, such as age, sex, ethnicity, or parents' education levels, usually determined through surveys or records. (pp. 116–117)

discovery learning A learning situation in which a learner is given a challenging problem, task, or project to carry out on his or her own. See also *collaborative learning*. (pp. 83, 86)

disordinal interaction An interaction between two variables in which the lines cross, exemplified when one instructional method is more effective for one kind of learner and another instructional method is more effective for another kind of learner. See also *ordinal interaction*. (p. 119)

dual channels principle A principle from the science of learning stating that people have separate channels for processing verbal and visual material. See also *limited capacity principle, active processing principle*. (pp. 30–31, 35, 46)

Ebbinghaus' learning curve See *learning curve*.

educational objective A moderately specific statement intended to guide curriculum development, such as "ability to read musical scores." See also *instructional objective, global objective*. (pp. 58–59)

effect size (d) A measure of the strength of an effect in an experiment, computed by subtracting the mean score of the control group from the mean score of the treatment group and dividing by the pooled standard deviation. See also *experiment*. (pp. 104–105, 107)

elaboration principle An evidence-based principle for studying by generating stating that people learn better when they outline, summarize, or elaborate on the presented material. See also *testing principle, self-explanation principle, questioning principle*. (p. 74)

error analysis Examining each learner's individual pattern of errors on a set of problems to determine whether the learner is systematically applying a faulty procedure. (pp. 114–115)

essential overload A learning scenario in which the required amount of essential processing and generative processing exceeds the learner's cognitive capacity. To address the problem of essential overload, an important instructional goal is to manage essential processing. See also *extraneous overload, generative underutilization*. (p. 64)

essential processing Basic cognitive processing during learning required to mentally represent the presented material, caused by the inherent complexity of the material. See also *extraneous processing, generative processing*. (pp. 62–65, 68–69)

evaluate An instructional objective that involves making judgments based on criteria or standards, such as judging which of two methods is best for solving a probability word problem. See also *remember, understand, apply, analyze, create*. (p. 61)

evidence-based learning theory The idea that learning theories should be testable and based on evidence. See also *science of learning, evidence-based practice*. (p. 18)

evidence-based practice The idea that instructional principles should be testable and supported by rigorous research findings. See also *evidence-based learning theory*. (pp. 54–55)

expectation principle An evidence-based principle for reducing extraneous processing stating that people learn better when they are shown in advance the type of test items they will receive following the lesson. See also *coherence principle, signaling principle, spatial contiguity principle, temporal contiguity principle*. (p. 66)

experiment A comparison between the performance of an experimental group and a control group in which the groups receive identical treatments except for the instructional manipulation (i.e., experimental control), the learners are randomly assigned to groups (i.e., random assignment), and the learners are tested on a relevant measure of learning (i.e., appropriate measures). Experiments are useful for determining the causal effects of an instructional method on learning outcomes (i.e., determining what works). See also *factorial experiment, observational analysis*. (pp. 100–101, 104–107)

experimental comparison See *experiment*.

expertise reversal effect An attribute treatment interaction involving prior knowledge in which instructional methods that are effective for low-knowledge learners are not effective or are even harmful for high-knowledge learners. See also *attribute treatment interaction*. (p. 121)

extraneous overload A learning scenario in which the learner needs to engage in extraneous processing, essential processing, and generative processing but only has sufficient cognitive capacity to support extraneous processing and perhaps a small amount of essential processing. To address the problem of extraneous overload, an important instructional goal is to reduce extraneous processing. See also *essential overload, generative underutilization*. (p. 64)

extraneous processing Cognitive processing during learning that does not support the objective of the lesson, caused by poor instructional design. See also *essential processing, generative processing*. (pp. 62–67)

factorial experiment An experiment that involves a comparison between an experimental group and a control group (as in an experiment) as well as one or more additional factors, such as type of learner, type of material, or type of learning environment. Factorial experiments are useful in determining the boundary conditions for instructional effects (i.e., determining when does it work)—such as whether an instructional method works best for certain kinds of learners, materials, or learning contexts. See also *experiment, observational analysis*. (p. 102)

facts Factual knowledge about the world, such as knowing "Boston is in Massachusetts." See also *concepts, procedures, strategies, beliefs*. (pp. 14, 17, 60)

factual knowledge See *facts*.

far transfer problem Solving a new problem that requires applying a new principle or method in a new situation. See also *retention problem, near transfer problem*. (pp. 108–109)

feedback principle An evidence-based principle for studying by practicing stating that people learn better from practice when they receive explanative feedback on their performance. See also *spacing principle, worked example principle, guided discovery principle*. (p. 72)

forgetting curve A quantitative functional relation between a measure of time since learning (usually on the *x*-axis of a graph) and a measure of learning outcome, such as test performance (usually on the *y*-axis of a graph). See also *learning curve*. (pp. 26–27, 47)

formative assessment Assessment conducted during instruction that is intended to determine what the learner is learning in order to adjust ongoing instruction. See also *pre-assessment, summative assessment*. (p. 95)

free recall list learning A learning task in which the learner receives one word at a time and is asked to recall them in any order, such as learning the 50 states in the United States. See also *serial list learning, paired-associate learning*. (p. 46)

general theory of learning A theory of learning that applies across all learning situations. See also *psychology of subject areas, minimodels of learning*. (p. 44)

general transfer Transfer in which there is nothing specifically in common between the learning task and the transfer task. See also *transfer, mixed transfer, specific transfer*. (p. 21)

generative effect The finding that people learn better when they engage in generative activities during learning, such as generating a summary sentence. See also *active learning*. (p. 33)

generative processing Deep cognitive processing during learning required to make sense of the presented material, caused by the learner's motivation to make an effort to learn. See also *extraneous processing, essential processing*. (pp. 62–65, 70–71, 74)

generative theory of learning A theory of learning by Merlin C. Wittrock, which proposes that people learn more deeply when they engage in learning strategies that prime appropriate cognitive processes during learning. See also *active learning*. (p. 33)

generative underutilization A learning scenario in which the learner has sufficient cognitive capacity to engage in generative processing but chooses not to do so. To address the problem of generative underutilization, an important goal is to foster generative processing. See also *essential overload, extraneous overload.* (p. 65)

global objective General statements intended to provide vision for educators, such as "All students will learn to be responsible citizens." See also *instructional objective, educational objective.* (pp. 58–59)

graphic organizer An instructional technique intended to guide the process of organizing, which involves a matrix or hierarchy or network that shows the key concepts in a spatial layout. See also *outline, headings, pointer words, organizing, signaling principle.* (pp. 78–79)

guided discovery principle An evidence-based principle for studying by practicing stating that people learn better when they receive guidance such as modeling, coaching, and scaffolding as they perform a task. See also *spacing principle, feedback principle, worked example principle.* (p. 72)

habit family hierarchy A mechanism of learning in which a learner is assumed to have a stimulus associated with a collection of responses, and the associations are of varying strengths based on prior rewards and punishments. See also *law of effect.* (p. 25)

headings An instructional technique intended to guide the process of organizing, which involves highlighted words at the start of each section that are keyed to the outline. See also *outline, pointer words, graphic organizer, organizing, signaling principle.* (pp. 78–79)

highlighting An instructional technique intended to guide the process of selecting, which involves emphasis on certain words by use of different font size, style, color, underlining, flashing, and so on. See also *objectives, pre-questions, post-questions, selecting, signaling principle.* (pp. 76–77)

information acquisition A view of how learning works, holding that learning involves adding presented information (such as "The three metaphors of learning are response strengthening, information acquisition, and knowledge construction") to the learner's memory. According to this view, the learner is a passive recipient of information, and the teacher is a dispenser of information. See also *response strengthening, knowledge construction.* (pp. 22–23, 26–27)

instruction The instructor's manipulation of the learner's environment in order to foster learning. Instruction is manipulating the learner's experiences with the intention to cause a change in the learner's knowledge. See also *learning, assessment, science of instruction.* (pp. 2, 4–5, 52–53)

instructional effects Determining whether a particular instructional method is effective (i.e., what works), the conditions under which it is effective (when does it work?), and the mechanisms that cause the effects (how does it work?). (pp. 98–107)

instructional method A way of manipulating the learner's environment that is intended to affect the learner's experience. See also *instruction, instructional effects.* (p. 52)

instructional objective A specification of an intended change in the learner's knowledge that includes a description of (1) what was learned, (2) how it is used, and (3) how to interpret the learner's performance. See also *global objective, educational objective.* (pp. 56–61)

instructional treatment See *instructional method.*

integrating A cognitive process required for meaningful learning in which the learner connects verbal and pictorial representations with each other and with prior knowledge activated from long-term memory. Integrating involves the transfer of knowledge from long-term memory to working memory, represented as an arrow from long-term memory to working memory. See also *selecting, organizing.* (pp. 37, 76, 80–81)

inter-rater reliability A form of objectivity involving the correlation between the scores of two scorers. See also *objectivity.* (p. 97)

knowledge construction A view of how learning works that describes learning as building a mental representation (such as a mental model of how learning works) from which the learner can make inferences. According to this view, the learner is an active

sense maker, and the teacher is a cognitive guide. See also *response strengthening, information acquisition, active learning.* (pp. 22–23, 28–29)

law of effect A principle of learning proposed by E. L. Thorndike as follows: "Of the several responses made to the same situation, those which are accompanied or closely followed by satisfaction to the animal will, other things being equal, be more firmly connected with the situation so that when it recurs, they will be more likely to recur; those which are accompanied or closely followed by discomfort to the animal will, other things being equal, have their connections with that situation weakened, so that, when it recurs, they will be less likely to occur." See also *habit family hierarchy.* (p. 25)

learning A change in knowledge attributable to experience. See also *instruction, assessment, science of learning.* (pp. 2, 4–5, 14–16, 52–53)

learning curve A quantitative functional relation between a measure of practice, such as time spent on learning (usually represented on the x-axis of a graph), and a measure of learning outcome, such as test performance (usually represented on the y-axis of a graph). See also *forgetting curve.* (pp. 24, 26, 47)

learning outcome A change in the learner's knowledge caused by instruction (i.e., what is learned). (pp. 93, 108–111, 114–115)

levels of processing The finding that people remember words better if they engage in deep processing of the words during learning. (p. 47)

leveling Forgetting or distorting specific details from presented material during remembering. See also *sharpening, rationalization.* (p. 29)

limited capacity principle A principle from the science of learning stating that people can process only small amounts of material in each channel at any one time. See also *dual channels principle, active processing principle.* (pp. 30, 32, 35, 46)

long-term memory A memory store that holds information in organized format, has large capacity, and lasts for long periods of time (many years). See also *sensory memory, working memory.* (pp. 34–38)

magic number 7 The finding that people can remember or attend to approximately seven chunks of information at one time. See also *limited capacity principle.* (p. 32)

meaningful learning A learning outcome indicated by good retention test performance and good transfer test performance. See also *rote learning, no learning, retention test, transfer test.* (pp. 110–113)

memory span The longest list a person can recall in order without error. See also *attention span, memory span effect, magic number 7.* (p. 32)

memory span effect The finding that people can remember approximately seven chunks of information on a memory span task. See also *memory span, magic number 7.* (p. 47)

metacognition Awareness and control of one's cognitive processing. In the context of learning, metacognition includes the learners' knowledge of how they learn (i.e., cognitive processing during learning) and the learners' control of the learning process (i.e., control of cognitive processing). See also *motivation.* (pp. 38, 42–43)

Miller's magic number 7 See *magic number 7.*

mini-models of learning Theories of learning that apply to specific laboratory tasks. See also *psychology of subject areas, general theory of learning.* (p. 44)

mixed transfer Transfer of a general principle or strategy from the learning task to the transfer task. See also *transfer, general transfer, specific transfer.* (p. 21)

modality principle An evidence-based principle for managing essential processing in which people learn better from a multimedia lesson when words are spoken rather than printed. See also *segmenting principle, pretraining principle.* (p. 68)

motivation An internal state that initiates and maintains goal-directed behavior. See also *metacognition.* (pp. 38–41)

multileveled posttest Administering a collection of posttests ranging from retention tests to transfer tests in order to compare each learner's pattern of performance across the posttests. (p. 115)

multimedia principle An evidence-based principle for fostering generative processing stating that people learn better from words and pictures than from words alone. See also *personalization principle, concretizing principle, anchoring principle.* (pp. 70–71)

near transfer problem Solving a new problem that requires applying the learned principle or method in a new situation. See also *retention problem, far transfer problem.* (pp. 108–109)

negative transfer A situation in which prior learning harms new learning or performance. See also *positive transfer, neutral transfer.* (p. 20)

neutral transfer A situation in which prior learning has no effect on new learning or performance. See also *positive transfer, negative transfer.* (p. 20)

no learning A learning outcome indicated by poor retention test performance and poor transfer test performance. See also *meaningful learning, rote learning, retention test, transfer test.* (p. 110)

norm-referenced test A test that gives a score that specifies where someone stands relative to other test takers. See also *criterion-referenced test.* (p. 97)

objectives An instructional technique intended to guide the process of selecting, which involves statements of what the learner should learn from the lesson. See also *pre-questions, post-questions, highlighting, selecting, expectation principle.* (pp. 76–77)

objectivity In testing, a form of reliability in which a test is scored the same way by all scorers. See also *validity, referencing, reliablity.* (pp. 96–97)

observational analysis A form of assessment that involves observing learners during a learning episode or administering an interview or questionnaire concerning what the learner was doing during learning; useful for determining the mechanism underlying instructional effects (i.e., determining how it works). See also *experiment, factorial experiment.* (p. 103)

one-way street A view of the relation between the science of learning and the science of instruction in which basic researchers create the science of learning and practitioners apply it. See also *dead-end street, two-way street.* (pp. 8–9)

ordinal interaction An interaction between two variables in which the lines do not cross, exemplified when one instructional method has a stronger effect for one kind of learner than for another kind of learner. See also *disordinal interaction.* (p. 119)

organizing A cognitive process required for meaningful learning in which the learner organizes selected words or pictures into a coherent mental representation. Organizing involves the manipulation of information in working memory and is represented as an arrow within working memory. See also *selecting, integrating.* (pp. 37, 76, 78–79)

outline An instructional technique intended to guide the process of organizing, which involves a sentence in the introduction that lists the sections of the lesson or a list of sections at the beginning of the lesson. See also *headings, pointer words, graphic organizer, organizing, signaling principle.* (pp. 78–79)

paired-associate learning A learning task in which the learner receives one word pair at a time and is asked to recall the second word in each pair when cued with the first word, such as learning foreign language vocabulary. See also *free recall list learning, serial list learning.* (p. 46)

Paivio's concreteness effect See *concreteness effect.*

Pasteur's Quadrant Research that is intended to contribute to theory and practice. See also *basic research on applied problems, use-inspired based research.* (p. 10)

percentile rank A form of standardizing involving the conversion of a test score into a number indicating the percentage of scores that are below the test score. See also *standard score, referencing.* (p. 97)

personalization principle An evidence-based principle for fostering generative processing in which people learn better when the instructor uses conversational style rather than formal style. See also *multimedia principle, concretizing principle, anchoring principle.* (p. 70)

picture superiority effect The finding that an item is remembered better if it is presented as a picture rather than a word. See also *concreteness effect, dual channels principle.* (p. 31)

pointer words An instructional technique intended to guide the process of organizing that involves words such as "first . . . second . . . third" or "in contrast" or "as a result." See also *outline, headings, graphic organizer, organizing, signaling principle.* (pp. 78–79)

positive transfer A situation in which prior learning improves new learning or performance. See also *negative transfer, neutral transfer.* (p. 20)

post-questions An instructional technique intended to guide the process of selecting that involves questions inserted after each section of a lesson for the learner to answer. See also *objectives, pre-questions, highlighting, selecting, questioning principle.* (pp. 76–77)

pre-assessment Assessment conducted before instruction intended to determine the characteristics of the learner in order to plan for appropriate instruction. See also *formative assessment, summative assessment.* (p. 95)

pre-questions An instructional technique intended to guide the process of selecting that involves questions inserted before each section of a lesson for the learner to answer. See also *objectives, post-questions, highlighting, selecting, questioning principle.* (pp. 76–77)

pretraining principle An evidence-based principle for managing essential processing in which people learn better from a complex lesson when they receive pretraining in the names and characteristics of the key concepts. See also *segmenting principle, modality principle.* (p. 68)

procedural knowledge See *procedures.*

procedures Step-by-step processes, such as knowing how to compute 252×12. See also *facts, concepts, strategies, beliefs.* (pp. 14, 17, 60)

psychology of subject areas Theories of how people learn school subjects such as reading, writing, mathematics, science, or history. See also *general theory of learning, mini-models of learning.* (pp. 44–45)

questioning principle An evidence-based principle for studying by generating in which people learn better when they must ask and answer deep questions during learning. See also *testing principle, self-explanation principle, elaboration principle.* (p. 74)

randomized controlled experiment See *experiment.*

rationalization Reorganizing presented material around a familiar theme during remembering. See also *leveling, sharpening.* (p. 29)

referencing A method of producing a test score that is interpretable. See also *validity, reliability, objectivity.* (pp. 96–97)

release from proactive interference The finding that people's memory performance declines for a word list that contains words from the same category, but recovers when they switch to a list of words from a new category. (p. 47)

reliability In testing, refers to the idea that a test score is consistent; that is, the same score is obtained every time under the same circumstances. See also *validity, objectivity, referencing.* (pp. 96–97)

remember An instructional objective that involves retrieving knowledge from long-term memory, such as, "State the formula for binomial probability." See also *understand, apply, analyze, evaluate, create.* (p. 61)

replication Conducting the same experimental comparison over again, perhaps with different lesson content, kinds of learners, or learning venues; useful in determining how far an instructional effect can generalize beyond the original experiment. See also *experiment.* (p. 105)

response strengthening A view of how learning works holding that learning involves strengthening or weakening of an association between a stimulus (such as, "What is 2 plus 2?") and a response (such as, "4"). According to this view, the learner is a passive recipient of rewards and punishments, and the teacher is a dispenser of rewards of punishments. See also *information acquisition, knowledge construction.* (pp. 22–25)

retention problem A problem that is the same or very similar to problems in the lesson. See also *near transfer problem, far transfer problem.* (pp. 108–109)

retention test A test that measures how much the learner remembers. See also *transfer test.* (pp. 108–109)

rote learning A learning outcome indicated by good retention test performance and poor transfer test performance. See also *meaningful learning, no learning, retention test, transfer test.* (pp. 110–113)

science of assessment The scientific study of how to determine what people know. See also *science of instruction, science of learning.* (pp. vii, 2–3, 94, 128)

science of instruction The scientific study of how to help people learn. See also *science of assessment, science of learning.* (pp. vii, 2–3, 8–11, 54–65, 128)

science of learning The scientific study of how people learn. See also *science of assessment, science of instruction.* (pp. vii, 2–3, 8–11, 18, 127–128)

segmenting principle An evidence-based principle for managing essential processing stating that people learn better when a complex lesson is presented in manageable parts. See also *pretraining principle, modality principle.* (pp. 68–69)

selecting A cognitive process required for meaningful learning in which the learner pays attention to relevant words and pictures from the presented material. Selecting involves the transfer of information from sensory memory to working memory and is represented as an arrow from sensory memory to working memory. See also *organizing, integrating.* (pp. 37, 76–77)

self-explanation principle An evidence-based principle for studying by generating stating that people learn better when they explain a lesson to themselves during learning. See also *testing principle, questioning principle, elaboration principle.* (pp. 74–75)

sensory memory A memory store that holds information in the same sensory format as presented, has large capacity, and lasts for a very brief time (i.e., less than 1 second). Spoken words impinging in the ears are held briefly as sounds in auditory sensory memory and printed words and pictures impinging on the eyes are held briefly as images in visual sensory memory. See also *working memory, long-term memory.* (pp. 34, 36–38)

serial list learning A learning task in which the learner receives one word at a time and is asked to recall them in order of presentation, such as memorizing the letters of the alphabet or the days of the week. See also *free recall list learning, paired-associate learning.* (pp. 26, 46)

sharpening Elaborating on certain crucial features from presented material during remembering. See also *leveling, rationalization.* (p. 29)

signaling principle An evidence-based principle for reducing extraneous processing stating that people learn better when the organization of a lesson is highlighted. See also *coherence principle, spatial contiguity principle, temporal contiguity principle, expectation principle.* (p. 66)

spacing principle An evidence-based principle for studying by practicing stating that people learn better when they spread out practice over several shorter sessions rather than massing practice in one longer lesson. See also *feedback principle, worked example principle, guided discovery principle.* (p. 72)

spatial contiguity principle An evidence-based principle for reducing extraneous processing stating that people learn better when corresponding printed words and pictures are near rather than far from each other on the screen or page. See also *coherence principle, signaling principle, temporal contiguity principle, expectation principle.* (pp. 66–67)

specific transfer Transfer of specific behaviors, facts, or procedures from the learning task to the transfer task. See also *transfer, general transfer, mixed transfer.* (p. 21)

split-half reliability A form of reliability involving the correlation between two halves of a test. See also *test-retest reliability, reliability.* (p. 97)

standard score A form of standardizing involving the conversion of a test score into the number of standard deviations above or below the mean. See also *percentile rank, referencing.* (p. 97)

state-dependent learning The finding that people remember a word list better if the testing situation is similar to the learning situation. (p. 47)

statistical power analysis Determines the number of participants needed to adequately conduct an experimental comparison. See also *experiment.* (p. 107)

strategic knowledge See *strategies.*

strategies General methods, such as knowing how to break a problem into parts. See also *facts, concepts, procedures, beliefs.* (pp. 14, 17, 60)

summative assessment Assessment conducted after instruction that is intended to provide accountability by documenting student learning or to provide input for program revision. See also *preassessment, formative assessment.* (p. 95)

temporal contiguity principle An evidence-based principle for reducing extraneous processing stating that people learn better when corresponding spoken words and pictures are presented simultaneously rather than successively. See also *coherence principle, signaling principle, spatial contiguity principle, expectation principle.* (p. 66)

testing principle An evidence-based principle for studying by generating stating that people learn better from taking a practice test rather than from restudying. See also *self-explanation principle, questioning principle, elaboration principle.* (p. 74)

test-retest reliability A form of reliability involving a correlation between two administrations of the test. See also *split-half reliability, reliability.* (p. 97)

Thorndike's law of effect See *law of effect.*

transfer The effect of prior learning on new learning or performance. See also *positive transfer, negative transfer, neutral transfer, general transfer, specific transfer, mixed transfer.* (pp. 20–21, 108–109)

transfer test A test that measures how well the learner can evaluate or use the learned material in a new situation. See also *retention test, transfer.* (pp. 108–111, 113)

two-way street A view of the relation between the science of learning and the science of instruction in which researchers test learning theory in authentic learning situations (thereby contributing to the science of learning) and test instructional principles that are grounded in theory (thereby contributing to the science of instruction). See also *dead-end street, one-way street.* (pp. 8–9)

type I error Concluding there is an effect when there is not. For example, $p < .05$ means there is less than a 5% chance of committing a type I error. See also *type II error.* (pp. 106–107)

type II error Concluding there is not an effect when there is. For example, $p < .05$ does not refer to type II error, but the chances of type II error may be far greater than 5%. See also *type I error.* (pp. 106–107)

understand An instructional objective that involves constructing meaning from instructional messages, such as, "Restate the formula for binomial probability in your own words." See also *remember, apply, analyze, evaluate, create.* (p. 61)

use-inspired basic research Research that is intended to contribute to theory and practice (e.g., to both the science of learning and the science of instruction); referred to as Pasteur's Quadrant. See also *basic research on applied problems.* (pp. 10–11)

validity The degree to which a test score is interpreted and used for an appropriate purpose. See also *referencing, reliability, objectivity.* (pp. 96–97)

Wittrock's generative effects See *generative effects.*

worked example principle An evidence-based principle for studying by practicing stating that people learn better when worked examples are presented before to-be-solved problems. See also *spacing principle, feedback principle, guided discovery principle.* (pp. 72–73)

working memory A memory story that holds information in an organized format, has limited capacity, and lasts for a short time (less than 1 minute) unless actively processed. See also *sensory memory, long-term memory, limited capacity principle.* (pp. 32, 34–38)

AUTHOR INDEX